Clear Grammar 2

Clear Grammar 2

Activities for Spoken and Written Communication

Keith S. Folse

Ann Arbor

THE UNIVERSITY OF MICHIGAN PRESS

Illustrations by Sang Eun Choi

Acknowledgments

I would like to thank the numerous professionals who gave their expert advice in the design of the grammar presentations and some of the activities used in this textbook. Among these professionals, I would especially like to acknowledge members of TESLMW-L (the materials writers group on the TESL-L electronic communication list) who offered suggestions. Both TESL-L and TESLMW-L have proven time and time again to be excellent sources of new teaching ideas and techniques.

Special thanks go to the professionals at ESL programs at the following schools who contributed ideas and suggestions for the design and content of this book: American Language Academy (Seattle), American Language Academy (Tampa), ELS (Seattle), Houston Community College, Loyola University (New Orleans), Oregon State University (Corvallis), San Francisco State University, Spring Hill College (Mobile, AL), Tulane University (New Orleans), the University of Central Florida (Orlando), the University of Monterrey (Mexico), the University of North Texas (Denton), the University of South Florida (Tampa), the University of Southern Mississippi (Hattiesburg), the University of Washington (Seattle), and Valencia Community College (Orlando).

Finally, I would like to thank the staff of the University of Michigan Press who have worked with me on this project, particularly Mary Erwin and Kelly Sippell.

Contents

To the Teacher

Clear Grammar 2 is part of a three-volume series of grammar books for beginning to low-intermediate level students of English as a second or foreign language. Book 2 covers grammar points for upper-beginning nonnative speakers of English, including articles, *be going to,* irregular past tense, *how* questions, adverbs of frequency, object pronouns, *one* and *other,* possessive, comparison and superlative, modals, and problem words.

Clear Grammar 1 contains presentations and exercises on basic grammar points such as the verb *to be,* regular verbs, simple question and negative forms, and prepositions. *Clear Grammar 3* continues this series with more difficult grammar points such as present perfect, infinitives vs. gerunds, and relative clauses.

Clear Grammar 2 contains exercises that provide relevant practice in the basic grammar points for beginning students of English as a second language (ESL). It assumes that the student has at least a fair reading and writing ability with the English alphabet. It is designed to be used by adult learners, that is, high school age and up. It is suitable for either intensive or nonintensive programs.

An important feature of this book is the number and variety of types of exercises included. Teachers and learners need a large number of practices. A plus of this book is that it contains approximately 140 exercises and activities. Furthermore, whenever possible, two smaller exercises have been included instead of one long exercise so that one may be done in class with the teacher's guidance and the other can be sent home for independent learning. A second advantage of this book is the variety of types of practice exercises and learning activities. For example, approximately 20 percent of the exercises are speaking or some type of interaction activities. Some grammar points can be practiced at the single-sentence level while other points may be learned better if seen within a larger context. (A pertinent example of this is unit 11, "Modals.")

A strong attempt has been made to provide engaging activities in addition to the traditional single sentences with one blank. To this end, the written exercises are proportionally divided between sentence-level exercises and multisentence- and dialogue-level activities. Therefore, the resultant structure of this book is approximately 20 percent speaking/interactive exercises, 40 percent single-sentence practices, and 40 percent multisentence or minidialogue activities.

These last figures clearly illustrate an extremely important difference between the Clear Grammar series and other grammar books. While some grammar ESL books have included some speaking activities and others have included a few multisentence exercises, the three books in this series make use of contextualized exercises where possible. These features represent current views toward the learning of grammar in a second language, namely, that speaking practice is as important as written practice and that some grammar points are more apparent to students when these points are seen within a real and somewhat longer context.

Clear Grammar 2 has six main goals:

1. to teach the basic grammar points necessary for beginning to upper-beginning ESL students;
2. to provide ample written practice in these structures at the single-sentence level as well as at the multisentence and dialogue levels;
3. to provide a wide array of practices at varying cognitive levels (i.e., not just knowledge and comprehension but also synthesis and evaluation);
4. to provide oral communication work practicing these structures through a variety of activities and games;
5. to provide ample opportunities for students to check their progress while studying these structures; and
6. to serve as a grammar reference that is written with language and terms that a beginning-level ESL student can understand without teacher assistance.

Clear Grammar 2 consists of thirteen units. Unit 1 is a review of the basic grammatical structures covered in *Clear Grammar 1*. Unit 13 is a review unit of the material in *Clear Grammar 2*. Each of the other eleven units covers a single grammar area, but sometimes a particular area may have several subdivisions. An example is unit 2, "Articles," in which indefinite articles *a* and *an* are covered along with five usages of the definite article *the*. Another example is unit 11, "Modals," which teaches various usages for nine modals.

The units may be done in any order. However, it is recommended that the general sequencing of the units be followed whenever possible. An attempt has been made to recycle material from one unit into following units where appropriate. For example, once past tense for irregular verbs has been covered, many of the sentences in subsequent exercises in other units include irregular past tense for further reinforcement. Because unit 11, "Modals," is longer than the other units, some teachers may find it advantageous to teach one or two of the modals in between the other units rather than teaching the whole modals unit in its entirety. This is recommended if students have had little or no exposure to modals and their basic meanings. However, for groups that already have some background with modals, teachers may find that the material is not so difficult and therefore not a great deal of time has to be spent on each modal.

Though a great deal of variety of material exists in the book, there is a general pattern within each unit. The units begin with some kind of grammar presentation. Sometimes this presentation is inductive; other times it is deductive. This presentation is then followed by a list of the most likely mistakes (i.e., potential problems) for each structure. This is followed by a series of written exercises arranged from least to most cognitively demanding. (Unit 11, "Modals," is set up slightly differently; however, its layout is easy to understand.) After the written work are one or more speaking activities. This is followed by a multiple choice quiz. At the end of each unit there is a review test.

A unique feature of all three volumes of the Clear Grammar series is the inclusion of Challenge Boxes. Each Challenge Box presents a single question that requires a higher level of knowledge and understanding of the particular grammar point. Sometimes the Challenge Box requires learners to analyze the most difficult item in the previous exercise. Other times the Challenge Box presents a new item that is more difficult than the items in the previous excercise. In both cases, the purpose of this activity is twofold: (1) to raise students' understanding of the grammar point by dealing with a very difficult question about the grammatical point, and (2) to motivate the better students who might not have been challenged sufficiently by the previous exercise.

General Lesson Format

1. Grammar Presentation

    These presentations vary in method. In some units, they are deductive; in others, inductive; and in others, consciousness raising. L2 learners have a wide range of learner styles and employ an even greater range of learner strategies. It is believed that having a variety of presentation types for the grammatical structures is therefore advantageous.

2. List of Potential Errors with Corrections

    In this section of the unit, there is a list of several of the most commonly made errors. Right after each error is the corrected form so that students can see not only what they should avoid but how it should be corrected. Our students represent a wide range of linguistic groups, and every effort has been made to take this into account in selecting which kinds of errors to include here.

3. Written Exercises

    Teachers and students want a large number of written exercises to allow for ample practice of the newly learned structure. The exercises have been sequenced so that the early exercises require only passive knowledge of the grammar point. For example, students circle one of two answers or put a check mark by the correct word. These exercises are followed by others that are more cognitively demanding and require active production of the language structure. In this way, students can comfortably move from passive knowledge to active production of a structure.

    The written exercises in this book are short enough to be done in a small amount of time, yet they are thorough enough to provide sufficient practice for the structure in question. These exercises may be done in class or as homework. Furthermore, they may be checked quickly either by individual students or by the class.

4. Speaking Activities

    Each unit has at least one (and often several) speaking activities. The instructions are clearly written at the top of the exercise. Students are often directed to work with a partner. In this case, it is important for the teacher to make sure that students do not see their partner's material ahead of time as this will not be conducive to facilitating speaking. (However, not all speaking activities are set up in this manner. See the directions for the individual exercises for further clarification.)

5. Multiple Choice Exercise

    Because students often have such a hard time with this particular format and because it is similar to the format found on many standardized language tests, each unit includes an eight-question multiple choice exercise. It is important to discuss not only why the correct answers are correct but also why the distractors are not correct.

6. Review Test

    Equally as important as the teaching of a given grammar point is the measurement of the learning that has taken place. To this end, the last exercise in every unit is a review test. This review test has several *very* different kinds of questions on it. For example, one kind of question may require a simple completion while another may require error identification. This variety allows all students an opportunity to demonstrate their knowledge without interference caused by the type of question.

Answer Key

In the back of the book, there is a section that contains the answers for all exercises in this text. These answers are provided so that students may check to see if their answers are correct. It is supposed that students will use the answer key after they have actually done the exercises. It is further hoped that students will use the answer key to detect their mistakes and then return to the exercises to discover the source of their error. The answer key also makes it possible for students engaged in independent study to use this workbook.

Grammar Terminology

In this book, grammar is not viewed as a theoretical science that requires complex terminology. Surely the main purpose of studying grammar in a foreign language is to be able to function better in that language, that is, to produce *accurate* communication (not just communication). To that end, the main focus of the presentations in this book is on being able to use English accurately and not on learning labels that are of little use. However, this does not mean that terminology is or should be avoided. Terms such as *adverbs of frequency* and *modals* are introduced and explained. However, grammar terminology is only introduced when it is necessary. Furthermore, when it is introduced, explanations have been simplified to reflect the level of the learner's English ability. Complex grammar terminology serves no justifiable purpose and is to be avoided at all costs in good ESL classes and materials.

Using This Book in Your Curriculum

The number of hours needed to complete this book depends to a large extent on the students in your class. A beginning-level group may need up to 60 hours to finish all the material, while a more advanced group might be able to omit certain units and do more work as homework, therefore using less class time. In this case, the students could finish the material in approximately 35 hours. The results of the diagnostic test (at the end of the book) can help you decide which units, if any, can be omitted or should be assigned as homework to certain students only in order to use group class time the most effectively.

Another factor that will greatly influence the number of class hours needed to complete this material successfully is whether or not the oral activities are done in class. It is recommended that teachers make every effort to do these speaking fluency activities in order to build up students' speaking ability and their confidence in their ability to use spoken English. An instructor in a course in which time is an important factor should consider ways of correcting student homework quickly (e.g., posting homework answer sheets on the wall) that are less time consuming rather than omitting the speaking fluency activities.

There is a diagnostic test at the back of the book. More information about this test is given in the next section. In order to make the best use of (limited) class time, the results of this test can guide you in choosing which units to cover and which units to omit if necessary.

About the Diagnostic Test

The diagnostic test is printed on perforated pages. Have the students remove this test and take it at the first class meeting. The test consists of twenty-four questions, two for each of the twelve units. (The thirteenth unit of the book is a review of the entire book, and thus no question matches it solely.) The test is set up in two parts, each part consisting of twelve questions. You may set your own time limit, but a recommended time limit is twenty minutes for all twenty-four questions. (Answers are not provided.)

The scoring for the test is fairly straightforward. On the test sheet, look to see for which units the student has missed both questions, for which the student has missed only one of the two questions, and for which the student has not missed either of the questions. You will need to make a composite picture of the results for your whole group. The units for which the most students have missed both questions or one question are the units that your class should focus on first.

Testing

Evaluation is extremely important in any language classroom, and it has a definite role in the grammar classroom. Frequent testing, not just major exams but small quizzes or checks, is vital to allow the learners to see what they have mastered and what still needs further work and to facilitate the teacher in gauging whether individual students have understood and retained the contents of the class.

Testing can come in many forms. Some teachers prefer cloze activities; others prefer multiple choice. Some teachers prefer discrete grammar items; others insist on context. Some include listening and/or speaking; others deal only with printed language. The most important things to keep in mind when testing are (1) students should know what kind of questions to expect, that is, they should know what they will have to do, because this affects how they should study, and (2) the test should test what was taught and nothing else. This second point is the mark of a good test and is essential to the fair treatment of the students.

About the Final Test

In addition to the diagnostic test, there is a final test on page 175. This is meant to be done toward the end of the course when most, if not all, of the book has been covered. This test is also printed on perforated pages and should be removed early in the course to prevent students from looking ahead. For this reason, some teachers will have students remove this test at the first class meeting and then collect these tests. It is not recommended that the results of this particular test be used as the sole deciding factor in whether a student moves from one level or course to the next. This is especially true if you have not had your students answer this type of question during the course. In general, this type of test is more difficult than regular multiple choice or cloze, and any student who scores at least 70 percent is probably ready to move on to *Clear Grammar 3*.

This test has two parts, each of which has the same directions. Students are to find the grammatical error in each sentence and correct it. Each of the two parts has twelve sentences, one sentence for each of the units in the book (except the final review unit, of course). The questions are in numerical order matching the corresponding units in the book. Thus, question number 7 in each part deals with material found in unit 7. It is possible to give the first part of this quiz as a progress check midway through the course and then to give the other half at the end to compare results. Again, it is not recommended that any decision regarding promotion to the next level of study be based solely on the results of this single exam.

Unit 1

Review of Book 1

1. negatives
2. *yes-no* questions
3. short answers
4. *wh-* questions
5. demonstrative words
6. quantity words
7. verb tenses
8. prepositions

Exercise 1.   Negatives. Write the correct form. Use each word in the box one time.

doesn't	isn't	didn't	don't	wasn't
don't	am not	didn't	wasn't	aren't

1. The children _____ watching TV now.

2. I _____ in New York City last year.

3. Small cars _____ use a lot of gasoline.

4. I _____ the oldest child in my family. My sister is older than I am.

5. Jim and Bill _____ eat pizza for dinner last night.

6. A Mercedes _____ cost less than $10,000.

7. It _____ rain very hard yesterday.

8. I bought a ticket from Miami to New York. It _____ very expensive.

9. People in Japan and Venezuela _____ speak the same language.

10. Egypt _____ in Asia.

1

Exercise 2. *Yes-No* Questions: *am, is, are, was, were, do, does, did*. Draw lines to make correct questions. Follow the example.

1. Was — Miami and Houston in Texas?

2. Did — New York have more people than Los Angeles?

3. Am — Vancouver the capital of British Columbia?

4. Do — the food at the party last night very good?

5. Are — Washington and Lincoln born in the U.S.?

6. Were — you make this cake yourself? It's delicious!

7. Is — I speak too quickly?

8. Does — I wrong?

Exercise 3. Short Answers: *am, is, are, was, were, do, does, did*. Write the possible short answers. Follow the example.

1. Does a Mercedes cost more than a BMW?

   Yes, __it does_____. OR No, __it doesn't_____.

2. Were you and your parents in Spain last summer?

   Yes, _____. OR No, _____.

3. Are blue and yellow your favorite colors?

   Yes, _____. OR No, _____.

4. Do people in that country eat rice every day?

   Yes, _____. OR No, _____.

5. Was the steak at that restaurant expensive?

   Yes, _____. OR No, _____.

6. Is blue your favorite color?

   Yes, _____. OR No, _____.

7. Am I sitting in your chair?

   Yes, _____. OR No, _____.

8. Did all of the students pass the test?

   Yes, _____. OR No, _____.

Exercise 4.　　*Wh-* Questions: *who,* what, where, when, why, which*. Make questions according to the underlined words. Follow the examples.

1. <u>Janet and Rick</u> went <u>to the party</u> <u>last night</u>.
　　　　A　　　　　　　　B　　　　C

(A) _Who went to the party last night?_ _____

(B) _Where did Janet and Rick go last night?_ _____

(C) _____

2. Melt means <u>change from solid to liquid</u>.

_____

3. <u>The red</u> car belongs to <u>John</u>.
　　　　A　　　　　　　　B

(A) _____

(B) _____

4. <u>Hydrogen</u> is the most abundant material in the universe. The chemical symbol of
　　　A

hydrogen is <u>H</u>.
　　　　　B

(A) _____

(B) _____

5. <u>Karen</u> called <u>Martha</u>. She called <u>because she wanted to borrow some money</u>.
　　　A　　　　　　B　　　　　　　　C

(A) _____

(B) _____

(C) _____

*Use *whom* in some sentences if your teacher tells you to do this.

Exercise 5.　　Demonstratives: *this, that, these, those.* Underline the correct word.

1. *(Bill is holding a small box in his hand. Mark is standing about ten feet away.)*

　　Mark:　　Bill, what is (this, that)?

　　Bill:　　(This, These) is a very old box. My dad gave it to me when I was only

　　　　　　seven.

(Bill opens the box and takes out some cards.)

Mark: What are (these, those, this, that)?

Bill: These are baseball cards. My dad bought them for me a long time ago.

2. *(Miss Williams teaches first grade at an elementary school. Her students are learning about different kinds of fruit. She has five different kinds of fruit on her desk. Miss Williams holds up one of the fruits.)*

Teacher: Class, what is (this, that)?

Susan: Is (this, that) an orange?

Teacher: No, it's not. Can anyone else guess?

Brian: Is (this, that) a grapefruit?

Teacher: Yes, this is a grapefruit. How many of you have eaten a grapefruit?

(About half of the students raise their hands.)

Teacher: OK, let's look at a different fruit.

(She holds up two mangoes.)

Teacher: Who knows what (this, that, these, those) are?

Maria: I know. Sometimes I eat them for dessert. (These, Those) are mangoes.

Teacher: Very good, Maria. So you like mangoes?

Maria: I love them. They're so sweet and juicy.

3. *(Joe and Bob are looking at shirts in a store. Bob is about five feet away from Joe.)*

Joe: Bob, can you help me? I need to buy a new blue shirt.

Bob: OK, let me look for a minute.

(Bob finds a nice blue shirt and picks it up.)

Bob: Hey, Joe, what about (this, that, these, those) shirt?

Joe: Maybe. How much is (that, those) shirt?

Bob: Let me see. The price is $22.50.

Joe: OK, I'll take it. Let's go to the register.

Exercise 6.   Quantity Words: *some, any, a few, a little, much, many, a lot of.*
Underline the correct word. For some, there is more than one
answer possible

1. *A:* Why are you going to the store now?

   B: I want to buy (some, any, much, few) cookies.

   A: We have (any, a lot, some, a little) cookies in the cabinet. Did you check?

   B: Yes, I did. There aren't (many, some, any) cookies. The jar is empty.

   A: It's already 9:30. Why do you need (much, some) cookies right now?

   B: I don't know. I just have this craving★ for (any, some) cookies. I'll be right back.

2. *A:* May I help you?

   B: Yes, I would like to buy (some, any, much, a little) vitamins.

   A: We have (a lot of, a little, any) different kinds of vitamins. What kind do you

       want?

   B: I don't really know. My doctor said I should start taking vitamins for my eyes.

   A: Well, we don't have (some, any, much, a little) vitamins just for eyes. I think you

       probably need a multipurpose vitamin.

   A: OK, that sounds good.

3. *A:* I'm going to make a chocolate cake. What do I need?

   B: You need (any, some) flour and (any, some) sugar.

   A: What about chocolate? What about peanuts?

   B: You need (any, some) chocolate, of course, but you

       don't need (any, some) peanuts.

   A: What about eggs? I'm going to buy a dozen.

   B: A dozen? No, you don't need (much, many) eggs

       to make a cake. You only need three or four.

   A: Can you think of anything else?

   B: Oh, yes, you need (a little, a few) baking powder

       and (any, some) butter.

★A craving is when you have a strong desire to eat or drink something. A craving is usually sudden or
unexpected. Some people have a craving for chocolate. Others have a craving for doughnuts. Just before you
go to bed at night, do you ever have a craving for one kind of food?

simple present

This action is true all of the time.
This action happens many times.

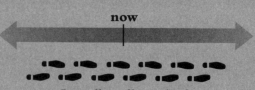

now

I usually walk to school.

present progressive

This action is happening now.

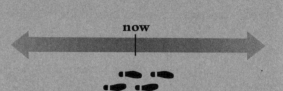

now

I am walking to school now.

simple past

This action is finished.
It happened one time or a few
times in the past.

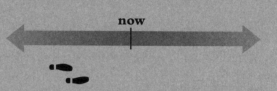

now

I walked to school yesterday.

Review: Verb Tenses and Time Words

Simple Present

This action is true all of the time.
This action happens many times.

I **am** a student.
The earth **moves** around the sun.
Sam **speaks** French and English.

Present Progressive

This action is happening now.

I **am studying** English.
The car **is moving** quickly.
Sam **is speaking** with his father.

Simple Past

This action is finished.
It happened in the past.

I **was** in Mexico in 1975.
Carol **lived** in an apartment last year.
Liam **went** home five minutes ago.
Mark and Joe **played** tennis last night.

Exercise 7. Verb Tenses. Follow the instructions in the box. Then check your answers with a partner.

We use certain time words with certain verb tenses. For example, we use *last night* with past tense, and we use *sometimes* with simple present. Read the list of fifteen time expressions. Put the time expressions with the correct verb tense. Follow the examples.

Simple Present	*Simple Past*	*Present Progressive*
every day	last night	

last night	always	at this moment	sometimes
every day	yesterday	the day before yesterday	this year
today	all the time	fifteen minutes ago	in 1980
this week	right now	now	

Exercise 8. Verb Tenses. Write the correct verb form on the line.

1. The early history of the United States is very interesting. Some people _____

   leave

   Europe in the 1600s. They _____ to this country for many different reasons.

   come

   Some people _____ religious freedom. Others _____ a chance for a

   want   desire

   better life. These people _____ colonies in this new land. Soon there

   start

   _____ thirteen colonies. Later these thirteen

   be

   colonies _____ the United States.

   become

2.   *(This is a postcard from Wendy to her sister Susan.)*

Dear Susan,

Hi, how _____ things at home? I hope everything _____ fine there.
　　　　　　be　　　　　　　　　　　　　　　　　　　　　　be

This _____ my first time in Honolulu, and I _____ it a lot. Today is
　　　be　　　　　　　　　　　　　　　　　　　　　like

such a beautiful day. Right now I _____ outside by the pool. The sun
　　　　　　　　　　　　　　　　　　sit

_____ and some birds _____ in the trees behind me. When I
shine　　　　　　　　　　　sing

_____ two days ago, it _____ a little cloudy, but there _____ any
arrive　　　　　　　　　be　　　　　　　　　　　　　be

clouds in the sky today. In the afternoon, I _____ shopping, and tonight I
　　　　　　　　　　　　　　　　　　　　　　go

_____ some special Hawaiian food for dinner. See you soon!
eat

　　　　　　　　　　　　　　　　　　　Love,
　　　　　　　　　　　　　　　　　　　Wendy

Speaking Activity (( ))

Exercise 9.   Speaking Activity: Past Tense of Regular and Irregular Verbs. Do student A OR student B. Do *one* of these only.

Step 1.   Number the left lines from 1 to 10 in any order. Mix up the numbers.
Step 2.   Fill in the right lines with the correct past tense of the verb. Check your answers with another student who did the same part (A or B) as you did.
Step 3.   Work with a partner who did not do the same part as you. Student A will read out all ten items as quickly as possible in numerical order. Student B must close the book and listen and then complete the items correctly. For example, student A will say, "I eat," and student B must say, "I ate." If this is correct, student A says, "That's correct." If this is not correct, student A says, "Try again" and repeats the item. When all the items are finished, student B will read out the other ten items.
Follow the examples.

　　　examples: he goes = he _went_____
　　　　　　　　John and Carol want = John and Carol _wanted_____

Student A

___. you are = you _____

___. the girl works = the girl _____

___. the cat sleeps = the cat _____

___. today is = today _____

___. Eric needs = Eric _____

___. Joe and Pam write = Joe and Pam _____

___. my car uses = my car _____

___. the boys play = the boys _____

___. dinner is = dinner _____

___. Toronto has = Toronto _____

Student B

___. he reads = he _____

___. Rachel calls = Rachel _____

___. the cats play = the cats _____

___. we see = we _____

___. the shoes cost = the shoes _____

___. the teacher says = the teacher _____

___. Brazil has = Brazil _____

___. the boy wakes = the boy _____

___. I get = I _____

___. the weather is = the weather _____

Speaking Activity

Exercise 10.   Speaking Practice

Step 1. Work with a partner. One of you is A, and the other is B. Each student should do only *one* of the two columns below.

Step 2. In your column (A or B), write the numbers 1 to 15 on the small lines on the left. Mix up your numbers. This is important.

Step 3. Next, read the sentence and write the negative of the verb on the line. Do not write out the whole sentence. If the sentence is "You are hungry," you should write *aren't* on the line because this is the negative of *are.*

Step 4. Take turns asking each other a question. Student A reads his or her number 1, and student B says the complete sentence again with the correct negative. If B's answer is correct, say "That's right." If it is not correct, ask the question again. Help your partner if he or she has any problems.

Student A

No.   *Negative Form*

___. You are tired.

_____

___. The men were late.

_____

Student B

No.   *Negative Form*

___. We played tennis all afternoon.

_____

___. Ali studied all night for the test.

_____

___. I speak French.

———————

___. I am hungry.

———————

___. You have my book.

———————

___. She works at the bank.

———————

___. You are a very good writer.

———————

___. Matt swims quickly.

———————

___. She is sick.

———————

___. They do the dishes by hand.

———————

___. We studied for the test.

———————

___. I played tennis with Maureen.

———————

___. Matt is a quick swimmer.

———————

___. He was here.

———————

___. Ken was late again.

———————

___. Today is Sunday.

———————

___. Tom likes coffee without sugar.

———————

___. Yesterday was Saturday.

———————

___. We were late for the party.

———————

___. You are a good cook.

———————

___. We worked from 9 to 5.

———————

___. I have a new car.

———————

___. I am worried about Lauren.

———————

___. The children were in the room.

———————

___. The grammar test was really easy.

———————

___. The questions were easy.

———————

___. She has a green bicycle.

———————

___. His name is Paul Smith.

———————

Exercise 11.   Multiple Choice: Verb Tenses. Circle the letter of the correct answer.

1. "Is Alice a good swimmer?"

   "I think she is an excellent swimmer. She _____ from 7 to 9 every morning and
   sometimes after school."

   (A) is swimming   (C) swim

   (B) swims   (D) swimming

2. "Janice _____ in a big house."

   "No, that isn't true. Janice lives in a small apartment."

   (A) lived   (C) live

   (B) lives   (D) was live

3. "This test is the last test. I am so happy!"

   "Me, too! I _____ tests!"

   (A) don't like   (C) didn't like

   (B) am not liking   (D) am not like

4. "How many computers _____ now?"

   "Two. One is a PC, and the other is a Macintosh."

   (A) are you owning   (C) own you

   (B) do you own   (D) you own

5. *Jim:*   "Did you and Tim go to the movies last night?"

   Todd: "Yes, we did."

   Jim: "What did you see?"

   Todd: "Well, I _____ to see *One More Week,* but Tim said it wasn't a good movie, so
           we decided to see *Dangerous Minds.*

   (A) want   (C) wanted

   (B) was wanting   (D) am wanting

6. "Let's go to the mall tomorrow. It's Saturday."

   "I can't. Every Saturday I _____ chess with Mike."

   (A) am practicing   (C) practiced

   (B) am practice   (D) practice

7. "How was the test?"

   "I _____ it. My score was only 42."

   (A) fail   (C) was going to fail

   (B) was failing   (D) failed

8. "How do you like your new class?"

   "It's hard. The teacher _____ really fast, so I can't understand the lesson sometimes."

   (A) talking   (C) talks

   (B) talk   (D) talked

────────

Exercise 12.   Prepositions: *at, on, in.* Write the correct preposition on the line.

1. *A:* Where is your math book?

   B: It's here _____ my bag.

   A: What time is your math class?

   B: It starts _____ 10 o'clock.

   A: Is your class near here?

   B: Yes, it is. It's _____ the second floor _____ Wilson Hall.

2. *A:* You don't look well. Why don't you go see a doctor?

   B: I have an appointment for later this afternoon.

   A: What time is your appointment?

   B: It's _____ 2:30.

   A: Where is the office?

   B: It's _____ Fowler Avenue. It's near the library.

3. *A:* What are you doing?

   B: Studying. My big biology test is _____ Tuesday.

   A: But today is only Thursday. You have five more days until the test.

   B: Dr. Jenkins's tests are tough.

   A: There's a party tonight _____ Pablo's house. Do you want to go?

   B: Thanks, but I think I'll stay _____ my room and study for this test.

   A: OK, but if you change your mind, let me know!

4. *A:* Where does your cat sleep?

   B: It sleeps _____ a box _____ the closet

   _____ my bedroom.

   A: So it sleeps _____ the house then?

   B: Yes, that's right.

5. *A:* I have a geography test _____ my first class tomorrow. Can you help me study?

   B: Sure. What do you want me to do?

   A: OK, here's a list of countries and their capital cities. Ask me questions about the

   location of the cities, and I'll tell you where they are.

   A: OK, where is Budapest?

   B: It's _____ Hungary.

   A: Where is Caracas?

   B: It's _____ Venezuela.

   A: What about Dakar?

   B: It's _____ Senegal.

   A: What time is your test tomorrow?

   B: It's _____ 7:00. Why?

   A: I think you should get some rest now. I don't think you need to study this

   material any more. You know it very well.

Unit 2

Articles

1. *a/an*
2. Ø (no article)
3. *the:* second reference
4. *the:* items familiar to speaker and hearer
5. *the:* only one
6. *the:* general vs. specific
7. *the:* geography words

**Thomas Jefferson was <u>an</u> important person
in U.S. history. He was <u>the</u> third president.**

A or An?

a	an
a book	an egg
a cat	an orange
a diamond	an article
a university	an umbrella
a house	an hour

1. Use **a** if the word begins with a **consonant★ sound**.
2. Use **an** if the word begins with a **vowel★ sound**.
3. Be careful with **h** and **u**. The letter **h** is sometimes silent (hour, honest).
   The letter **u** sometimes sounds like the letter **y** (university, union).

a	an
a green book	an interesting story
a small diamond	an expensive book

Adjectives (green, small, interesting, expensive) follow the same rules.

1. Use **a** if the word begins with a **consonant★ sound**.
2. Use **an** if the word begins with a **vowel★ sound**.

★vowel = **a, e, i, o, u**; consonant = all others (**b, c, d, f, g,** etc.)

CAREFUL! Watch out for these common mistakes.

1. Use **an** before vowel sounds. Do not use **a**.

   wrong: A apple has many vitamins.

   correct: An apple has many vitamins.

   wrong: It's raining. Don't forget to take a umbrella with you!
   correct: It's raining. Don't forget to take an umbrella with you!

2. Don't use **a** before words that begin with silent **h** or with the short sound of **u** as in *uncle* or *ugly*. Remember that we use **an** before vowel sounds. Pay attention to the sound, not just the letter.
   wrong: It takes a hour to drive from my house to the beach.
   correct: It takes an hour to drive from my house to the beach.

   wrong: Harvard is an university in the U.S.
   correct: Harvard is a university in the U.S.

   wrong: What is this letter? Is it a **E** or a **F**?
   correct: What is this letter? Is it an **E** or an **F**?

3. Don't use **a** or **an** with plural words.
   wrong: They are an interesting books.
   correct: They are interesting books.

   wrong: An elephants are extremely large animals.
   correct: Elephants are extremely large animals.

4. Don't use **a** or **an** if there is no noun.
   wrong: This is a blue.
   correct: This is a blue book.
               OR This is blue.
               OR This book is blue.

   wrong: It is an expensive.
   correct: It is expensive.
               OR It is an expensive car.
               OR This car is expensive.

5. Don't use a singular count noun without an article. For many nonnative speakers (especially those whose first language does not have indefinite articles), this is the most common error.

wrong: She has new car.
correct: She has a new car.

wrong: All the students made score of 70 or higher.
correct: All the students made a score of 70 or higher.

Exercise 1.   Write *a* or *an* on the line. Follow the examples.

1. _a_ test	11. ____ woman	21. ____ car
2. _an_ orange	12. ____ restaurant	22. ____ uncle
3. ____ class	13. ____ umbrella	23. ____ kitchen
4. ____ student	14. ____ hour	24. ____ elephant
5. ____ potato	15. ____ answer	25. ____ igloo
6. ____ pen	16. ____ exam	26. ____ blackboard
7. ____ year	17. ____ university	27. ____ snake
8. ____ ant	18. ____ ice cream cone	28. ____ oven
9. ____ egg	19. ____ E	29. ____ family
10. ____ K	20. ____ H	30. ____ X

CHALLENGE A student says the answer for 13, 17, and 22 is *an* because they all begin with the same letter (u). Is this correct? Why or why not? You are the teacher now. How do you answer this question?

Exercise 2.   Write *a* or *an* on the line. (*Note:* These phrases have an adjective before the noun, but the same rules for *a/an* apply.) Follow the example.

1. _an_ active person	6. ____ young boy	11. ____ orange car
2. ____ hard question	7. ____ delicious dinner	12. ____ English test
3. ____ university class	8. ____ very difficult test	13. ____ honest person
4. ____ aggressive animal	9. ____ ugly painting	14. ____ huge house
5. ____ very aggressive animal	10. ____ horrible test	15. ____ good parent

Exercise 3.   Read the sentences. Write *a*, *an*, or — on the line. Follow the examples.

1.   __—__ red __—__ is _a_ bright __—__ color.

2.   ___ elephant ___ is ___ large___ animal with ___ long nose and ___ big ears.

3.   ___ snake ___ doesn't ___ have ___ legs ___ or ___ arms.

4.   ___ gray ___ is ___ interesting ___ color ___ for ___ house.

5.   ___ onion ___ is ___ common ___ vegetable.

6.   ___ I ___ ate ___ egg ___ sandwich ___ with ___ mayonnaise ___ and ___ piece ___ of ___ cheese ___ yesterday.

7.   ___ tennis ___ racket ___ is ___ great ___ idea ___ for ___ birthday ___ present ___ for ___ tennis ___ player.

8.   What ___ is ___ good ___ name ___ for ___ cat?

9.   ___ every ___ kitchen ___ has ___ refrigerator ___ and ___ stove.

10. ___ tiger ___ is ___ strong ___ animal ___ with ___ striped ___ body ___ and ___ sharp ___ teeth.

The

This section will discuss five uses for *the*:

Usage No. 1.   Second reference
Usage No. 2.   Familiar to speaker and hearer
Usage No. 3.   Only one
Usage No. 4.   General vs. specific
Usage No. 5.   Geography words

Usage No. 1 for *The:* Second Reference

I went shopping yesterday. I bought

<u>a cake</u> and <u>some cheese</u>. I ate **the** cake
　1st　　　　1st　　　　　　2nd
for dessert, and tomorrow I'm going to

use **the** cheese to make cheeseburgers.
　　　2nd
The cheese was not expensive, but
　　3rd
the cake was pretty expensive.
　　3rd
Use **the** for the second (and subsequent) time you talk about something.

1st time:	a cake	some cheese
2nd time:	the cake	the cheese
3rd time:	the cake	the cheese
more times:	the _____	the _____

Exercise 4.   Write *a, an, the,* or — on the line. Follow the examples.

1. *Bob:*   Did you have __a__ test yesterday in math class?

    Sue: Yes, I did. And _the_ test was really difficult!

2. *Ann:*   I bought ___ pizza and ___ candy bar.

    Zina: What are you going to eat first?

    Ann: I love chocolate, so I'm going to eat _____ candy bar first.

    Zina: And what about _____ pizza?

    Ann: Oh, that's for later.

3. *Ann:*   This is _____ nice apartment. I think you should take it.

    Zina: Hmmm . . . maybe. It has _____ large kitchen and _____ small patio area.

    Ann: Yes, _____ kitchen is very large. It has _____ nice refrigerator and _____

                 microwave oven.

    Zina: I really like _____ kitchen, too.

    Ann: And _____ patio is nice. It's small, but I like _____ patio. So what's your

                 decision?

4. *Teacher:*   Everyone has _____ test paper now, right?

    Students: Yes.

    Teacher: OK, at the top of _____ paper, there are 2 small boxes. There's _____ box on

                 the left and _____ box on the right. In _____ left box, write your full name.

    Sue: Mr. Miller, do I write my first name or my last name in _____ box?

    Teacher: Sue, you didn't listen very well. Write your FULL name in _____ box.

                 Now does everyone understand what to write in _____ left box? OK,

                 write today's date in the right box.

    Pam: Mr. Miller, what is _____ date?

    Teacher: Here, I'll write _____ date on the blackboard. *(teacher writes the date)*

5. *Carl:*   What did you do _____ yesterday?

    Alan: Nothing special. I went shopping.

    Carl: What did you buy?

    Alan: I bought _____ cake and some cheese. I ate _____ cake for dessert, and

                 tomorrow I'm going to use _____ cheese to make _____ cheeseburgers.

                 _____ cheese was not expensive, but _____ cake was pretty expensive.

Exercise 5.   Write *a, an, the,* or — on the line. Follow the examples.

1. *Bob:*   Did you have __a__ test yesterday in math class?

   Sue: Yes, I did. And _the_ test was really difficult!

2. *Ann:*   What did you do last night?

   Zina: I went to see _____ movie.

   Ann: What was _____ movie?

   Zina: *All My Heart.*

   Ann: So it was _____ love story?

   Zina: That's right.

3. *Wes:*   I ate at that new restaurant on Main Street last night.

   Pete: Really? How was it?

   Wes: I liked it.

   Pete: What did you eat?

   Wes: I had _____ big salad and _____ double cheeseburger.

   Pete: Well, how was everything?

   Wes: _____ salad was very good. They give you a lot of tomatoes, and _____

   tomatoes were very fresh.

   Pete: That sounds good. I like to begin my dinner with _____ small salad.

   Wes: And _____ cheeseburger was great! You can't believe how much cheese

   they put on _____ cheeseburger. And _____ cheese was cheddar, and

   that's my favorite.

   Pete: Stop! My mouth is watering!

4. *Rick:*   Wow, I can't believe how crowded that store was!

   Ken: Gosh, I agree. Hey, can you help me put away these groceries?

   Rick: Sure. Just tell me where things go.

   Ken: OK, take everything out of the bags.

   Rick: Here's _____ box of cereal.

   Ken: Put _____ cereal in the top cabinet.

   Rick: Here's a bag of sugar.

   Ken: Put _____ sugar next to _____ cereal.

   Rick: Here's a bag of chicken wings.

Ken: Put _____ chicken wings in the refrigerator.

Rick: And what about these four cans of tuna?

Ken: Put them in the top cabinet, too, next to _____ cereal and _____ sugar.

Rick: OK, I'm finished.

Ken: Thanks for your help. Are you hungry?

Rick: Actually, yes, I am.

Ken: How about _____ sandwich?

Rick: OK, I need some bread.

Ken: _____ bread is in that brown box next to the refrigerator.

Rick: OK, thanks. Here it is.

Usage No. 2 for *The:* Familiar to Speaker and Hearer

Bob:	Hey, where's **the** newspaper?	the newspaper = there is only one
Ann:	It's over there on **the** sofa.	the sofa = there is only one; it's a sofa that both Bob and Ann know
Bob:	OK. I have it now.	
Ann:	Bob, I'm going to **the** store. Do you need anything?	the store = it's a store that Bob and Ann both know

Use **the** for something that the speaker and the hearer both know about or are familiar with. Sometimes **the** means that the hearer and the speaker are talking about the exact same object. When someone says "I passed the test," it means that the speaker and the hearer know which test the speaker is talking about.

Exercise 6.   Write *a, an, the,* or — on the line. Follow the examples.

1. *Bob:*   What's Sue doing?

   Jim: She's studying for __—__ tomorrow's test.

   Bob: Where is she studying?

   Jim: She's at __the__ library.

2. *Mike:*   Where can I buy _____ canned tuna?

   Carol: I'm going to _____ supermarket now. Do you want me to get a few cans for you?

3. *Greg:*   I'm thirsty.

    Bill: There's _____ 2-liter bottle of cola in _____ refrigerator.

    Greg: OK, thanks. Where can I find _____ glass?

    Bill: Look in _____ cabinet above _____ stove.

    Greg: Do you want something to drink, too? I can get _____ glass for you.

    Bill: No, thanks. I'm not very thirsty right now.

4. *Neal:*   Hey, it's 4:30, time for _____ game.

    Pam: I want to see _____ game, too. Turn on _____ TV.

    Neal: Oh, no! I can't find _____ remote control. Where is it?

    Pam: Is that it under _____ sofa? How did it get under there?

5. *Ricky:*   Kevin, where is _____ newspaper? I want to see if there is _____ good

              movie on TV tonight.

    Kevin: It's on _____ floor next to _____ TV.

6. *Ivan:*   Where can I buy _____ new tennis racket?

    Mark: You need to go to _____ sporting goods store.

    Ivan: Yes, but which one? I don't have a lot of _____ money.

    Mark: What about _____ sporting goods store on Simon Street?

    Ivan: Oh, yeah, you mean McHenry's, right?

    Mark: Yes, that's it. Their things are usually pretty cheap.

    Ivan: Good, because I don't have much money.

    Mark: Well, I have _____ old racket and you can have it.

    Ivan: Are you sure?

    Mark: Definitely. It's in _____ hall closet. Look on _____ top shelf.

Usage No. 3 for *The:* Only One

During an eclipse, don't look at **the** sun.	There's only one sun. (There are many eclipses.)
Joe: What's wrong with your car? *Bob:* There's a problem with **the** battery.	A car has only one battery.
He's **the** team captain.	A team has only one captain.
Please sit on **the** sofa.	Most homes have only one sofa.

A: Wow, that was a great movie. What
   did you think?
B: I liked **the** ending a lot.   A movie has only one ending.

A: What's your last name?
B: Michaelson. Why?
A: Wow! You and I have **the** same   Always use **the** with **same:** the same name.
   last name.

The third★ class has twenty-seven   Specific: there is only one class in the
students.   third position.

A: Class, can anyone name **the** parts
   of a TV?
B: **The** screen, **the** knobs, **the** cord, **the**   Use **the** for the parts of something.
   plug.

A: What's wrong?   Do not use **the** for parts of the body.
B: I cut my hand and I hurt my thumb.   Use possessive adjectives (**my, your,** etc.)

Note: Use **the** when there is only **one** of that thing.

★Use **the** with the first person, the second floor, the third day, the fourth time, the fifth week, etc.
Do not use **the** with question number one, door number two, gate number seven, etc.

Exercise 7.   Write *a, an, the,* or — on the line. Follow the examples.

1. *Jim:*   How many Canadians won __a__ gold medal in

                the last Olympic Games?

   Sue: I'm not sure. I know Jill Caruthers won __the__

                100-meter freestyle race.

2. *Bill:*   Who was _____ first person to walk on _____ moon?

   Ani: I think it was _____ Neil Armstrong.

3. *Jill:*   It's hot in this room. Is something wrong with _____ air conditioner?

   Ken: Yes, _____ thermostat is broken.

   Jill: What's _____ thermostat?

   Ken: It's _____ switch that controls _____ temperature in this room.

   Jill: Can you fix it?

   Ken: Well, we called _____ repair shop, and they sent someone here. He said

                that he has to get _____ new switch, and then he'll come back to fix it.

4. *Ed:*   What time does _____ first show start?

    Luke: At 4:15. Do you want to go?

    Ed: That's too early for me. When is _____ next movie?

    Luke: At 7:30. How's that?

    Ed: That's perfect for me.

5. *Pam:*   Guess what happened in my English class today.

    Maria: I don't know. What?

    Pam: In _____ middle of class, _____ teacher suddenly shouted as loud as she
               could.

    Maria: Why did she do that?

    Pam: We were reading _____ play by Shakespeare, and she wanted us to
               experience the words of the play.

    Maria: So what happened?

    Pam: Well, _____ students suddenly came to life. Everyone was paying atten-
               tion to _____ teacher and _____ words of _____ play.

    Maria: So it sounds pretty successful then.

6. *Elly:*   Who was _____ first person to sail around _____ world?

    Ann: I think it was _____ Magellan from _____ Portugal.

Usage No. 4 for *The:* General vs. Specific

I like apples, but I don't like **the** apples in this bag.

Use **the** for specific nouns when there is a phrase after them: the books **in this box,** the history **of Russia.**

I like history, especially modern Asian history.
But I don't like **the** history of early Asia.

the **NOUN** of **NOUN**

Shakespeare wrote in **the** sixteenth century.

Do not use **the** with people's names; use **the** with time periods.

A: I like this book. It's a very good book.
B: Is that the book that John gave you?
A: Yes, it is.

general meaning
the **NOUN** that **SUBJECT** + **VERB**

A: What do you like to eat as a snack?
B: Cheese is good.

All kinds of cheese are good. (general)

A: Look at all this food! What a great party!

B: Yeah, Sam really did a good job with this.

A: What do you recommend? What's good?

B: Well, **the** cheese is good.   This cheese on the table at this party is good. (specific)

Do not use **the** when you talk about something in general. Use **the** with very specific things, especially with nouns that are followed by **OF + NOUN** (I don't know the name of the book) or by **THAT + SUBJECT + VERB** (I like the car that John has).

Do not use **the** with: languages, sports, games, or school subjects.

Do not use **the** with: God, life, education, people's names, work (= office).

When we mean a category of something, we can use a plural count noun (I like cats) or a noncount noun (I like cheese). We do not use **the**.

Exercise 8.   Write *a, an, the,* or — on the line. Follow the examples.

1. *Ann:*   What is Alabama?

    Jo: It's __a__ state in the United States.

    Ann: Where is Alabama located?

    Jo: It's in _the_ southern part of the United States.

2. *Bob:*   So what are your plans after you finish _____ high school?

    Dan: I want to attend _____ university.

    Bob: Where would you like to go?

    Dan: I might go to _____ North Texas State University or _____ University of

             Texas. I'm also considering _____ San Francisco State University and

             _____ University of California at Los Angeles.

3. *Jill:*   What languages can you speak?

    Luke: I can speak _____ French and _____ Italian well, and I can read _____

             Dutch.

    Jill: Wow, that's great! Which of the three was _____ most difficult for you?

    Luke: I think _____ Dutch was _____ biggest problem for me. I don't know

             why, but it was really tough.

4. *Irene:*   Beth, I'm studying _____ English proverbs. Can you help me?

    Beth: Sure, what's your question?

    Irene: What do English speakers mean when they say "_____ time is _____ money"?

    Beth: I think they mean that _____ time is very valuable to them. You should not waste _____ time.

    Irene: And do you know _____ golden rule in English?

    Beth: Yes, in _____ simple English, it's "don't do something to someone that you would not want that person to do to you." It just means that we should treat _____ people as we want them to treat us.

5. *Hank:*   Do you like _____ apples?

    Fran: Yes, I do. Why?

    Hank: I bought some apples yesterday. Would you like one? *(he gives her an apple)*

    Fran: Thanks. They look delicious.

    Hank: They are. They're _____ Washington apples. I think they're _____ best apples.

6. *Jim:*   May I have your ticket please?

    Bob: Here you are.

    Jim: OK, Mr. Miles, everything is OK. _____ flight will depart at 7:35. Please be at _____ gate at least 30 minutes ahead of time.

    Bob: Thank you very much.

CHALLENGE   One student says the answer for the last blank above is *a* because gate is a singular count noun and must have the word *a* in front of it. This is wrong. You are the teacher. How can you explain this answer to the student?

Usage No. 5 for *The:* Geography

Last year I went to Japan and Singapore, but next year I'm going to **the** Philippines. **The** Netherlands is in Europe. We visited Switzerland in winter.★	Don't use **the** with countries or continents. If there is an **s** (plural) or the words union, republic, or united, use **the**. Canada, Great Britain, Nigeria (no **the**) the Dominican Republic, the U.S., the former Soviet Union (use **the**)
I'm staying at the Hilton Hotel near **the** art museum.	Use **the** with buildings such as hotels, restaurants, and museums.
The Panama Canal connects **the** Pacific Ocean with **the** Caribbean Sea.	Use **the** with most bodies of water.
The Andes are in South America.	Use **the** with mountain chains.
The Gobi Desert is very large.	Use **the** with deserts.

Some places require **the** and some don't.
• **the:** places that end in **s** (plural) or have the words **united, union, kingdom,** or **republic;** most buildings; most bodies of water (except lakes); mountain chains; deserts
• no **the:** cities, states, countries, continents; lakes

★The seasons do not require **the.** It is optional. (I like summer. He prefers the fall.)

Exercise 9.   Write *a, an, the,* or — on the line. Follow the examples.

1. — Hawaii	11. ____ Mississippi (= the river)	21. ____ Greece
2. the Hawaiian Islands	12. ____ Mississippi (= the state)	22. ____ North America
3. ____ Green Street	13. ____ United Kingdom	23. ____ Andaman Sea
4. ____ Louvre	14. ____ Lake Michigan	24. ____ Argentina
5. ____ Japan	15. ____ Himalaya Mountains	25. ____ Quebec
6. ____ Japan and China	16. ____ Caribbean Sea	26. ____ Asia
7. ____ Venezuela	17. ____ Intercontinental Hotel	27. ____ United Arab Emirates
8. ____ Africa	18. ____ Orinoco River	28. ____ Atlas Mountains
9. ____ Pacific Ocean	19. ____ Dead Sea	29. ____ Mojave Desert
10. ____ United Nations	20. ____ Dominican Republic	30. ____ Gulf of Mexico

Exercise 10. Write *a, an, the,* or — on the line. Follow the examples.

1. _—_ Boston

2. _—_ Washington, DC

3. _the_ Nile

4. ____ Mediterranean Sea

5. ____ Soviet Union

6. ____ Rome

7. ____ Rome and Athens

8. ____ Louvre

9. ____ Missouri River

10. ____ Finland

11. ____ Metropolitan Museum of Art

12. ____ British Columbia

13. ____ Kingdom of Saudi Arabia

14. ____ Saudi Arabia

15. ____ Tate Gallery

16. ____ Republic of Colombia

17. ____ Hilton Hotel

18. ____ St. Lawrence River

19. ____ Gulf of Mexico

20. ____ Atlantic Ocean

21. ____ Lake Geneva

22. ____ Amazon River

23. ____ Mexico

24. ____ Mexico City

25. ____ Honolulu

26. ____ Sahara

27. ____ Alps

28. ____ McDonalds

29. ____ Lake Titicaca

30. ____ New Zealand

Exercise 11. Language Comparison. What does your language do with articles? Translate each of these sentences into your own language. Pay attention to the underlined part. What happens to this underlined part in your language? When you have finished, discuss your answers with a partner or as a group.

English Sentence	*Your Language*
1. I have <u>a lemon</u> and <u>an apple</u>. <u>The lemon</u> is yellow, and <u>the apple</u> is red.	
2. *A:* John, can I use your telephone? *B:* Sure, it's in <u>the bedroom</u>.	
3. We get our paycheck at the <u>end of each month</u>.	
4. *A:* Do you like <u>literature</u>? *B:* Yes, I love <u>French literature</u>.	
5. Last year I visited <u>the pyramids</u> in <u>Egypt</u>.	

6. *A:* What did you do last night?
   B: I went to a party.
   A: So how was it?
   B: The party last night was great!
   A: Really? How was the food?
   B: It was wonderful.
   A: I'm sorry I didn't go. I had
         to work.
   B: Well, you know I love pizza....
   A: Yes, that's right.
   B: Well, the pizza was the best!

Discussion: What things are the same in English and your language?
                 What things are different?
                 If you are in a multilingual class, which languages are the most similar for
                 these six items?

Speaking Activity

Exercise 12a.   Speaking Activity: Information Chart—Student A

Step 1.   Work with a partner. Student A works on page 29. Student B works on
             page 30.
Step 2.   This chart lists well-known sites all over the world. It gives their locations
             and some facts about them. Your chart is missing some of the informa-
             tion, but your partner has this information. Take turns asking questions to
             complete this chart.
Step 3.   When both of you have finished,
             then you should compare books.
             Do not let your partner see your
             book until you have finished this
             activity.

             examples: Where is the Louvre?

                            How much does the
                            Statue of Liberty weigh?

                            What is the name of the
                            longest river in Africa?

Famous Sites	Location	Facts
the Empire State Building	New York City	• _____ tall • 102 floors
the Louvre	_____	• over a million pieces of art
Ottawa	Canada	• _____
the Andes Mountains	South America	• tallest mountains are _____ _____
the Mississippi River	_____	• 2,340 miles long
Mexico City	Mexico	• 15,000,000 people
the _____	Egypt	• _____ miles long • the longest river in Africa
the Eiffel Tower	Paris	• built in _____ • 904 feet high
the Statue of Liberty	_____ _____	• _____ feet high • _____ pounds • built in 1884

Speaking Activity

Exercise 12b. Speaking Activity: Information Chart—Student B

Step 1. Work with a partner. Student B works on this page. Student A works on page 29.

Step 2. This chart lists well-known sites all over the world. It gives their locations and some facts about them. Your chart is missing some of the information, but your partner has this information. Take turns asking questions to complete this chart.

Step 3. When both of you have finished, then you should compare books. Do not let your partner see your book until you have finished this activity.

examples: How long is the Mississippi River?
When was the Statue of Liberty built?
What is the second reason that the Nile is well known?

Famous Sites	*Location*	*Facts*
the Empire State Building	New York City	• 1,250 feet tall • _____ floors
the Louvre	Paris	• _____ pieces of art
_____	Canada	• capital of Canada
the Andes Mountains	_____	• tallest mountains are 20,000 feet
the Mississippi River	the central U.S.	• _____ miles long
Mexico City	Mexico	• _____ people
the Nile River	_____	• 4,145 miles long • _____
the Eiffel Tower	Paris	• built in 1889 • _____ feet high
the Statue of Liberty	on Ellis Island in New York City	• 301 feet high • 450,000 pounds • built in _____

Exercise 13.   Multiple Choice. Write the letter of the correct answer on the line.

1. I was born in _____.

    (A) Philippines   (C) United States

    (B) the Soviet Union   (D) the America

2. "What did you do last night?"

    "We watched _____ about life on another planet."

    (A) a movie   (C) the movie

    (B) any movie   (D) one movie

3. "I'm going to _____. Do you want anything?"

    "No, I don't need anything, but thanks for asking."

    (A) store   (C) a store

    (B) the stores   (D) the store

4. "Where can I put this box?"

    "How about over there on _____?"

    (A) the sofa   (C) a sofa

    (B) sofa   (D) sofas

5. "Do you know the answer to _____?"

    "No, I don't."

    (A) second question   (C) number the two

    (B) the second question   (D) the number two

6. One country I would really like to visit is the _____.

    (A) Switzerland   (C) Netherlands

    (B) Australia   (D) Argentina

7. I want to visit _____.

    (A) Dead Sea   (C) United Kingdom

    (B) Louvre   (D) Venezuela

8. "Do you read a lot?"

    "Yes, I do. I'm reading a very good book now. _____ is *Jungle*."

    (A) The title of a book   (C) The title of the book

    (B) A title of a book   (D) A title of the book

▬▬▬▬
Exercise 14.   Review Test

Part 1. Read this short passage. Fill in the blanks with *a, an, the,* or —.

_____ South Carolina is _____ small
state in _____ southeastern U.S. _____
state is shaped like _____ small triangle.
_____ North Carolina lies to the north,
and _____ Georgia lies to the southwest.
_____ Atlantic Ocean lies to the southeast.
With _____ population of _____ 3.5
million, _____ South Carolina ranks 25th.

About half of the people in _____ South Carolina live in _____ cities. _____ largest city is
_____ Columbia, which is also _____ capital. Another important city is _____ Charleston.

_____ South Carolina is _____ famous for _____ several things. _____ South Carolina
is _____ important manufacturing and farming state. One of its most important crops is
_____ tobacco. Many important battles of _____ American Revolution took place in
_____ South Carolina. In addition, on _____ December 20, 1860, _____ South Carolina
became _____ first state to leave _____ U.S. _____ Four months later, _____ Civil War
between _____ northern states and _____ southern states began in _____ Charleston.

Part 2.   Read each sentence carefully. Look at the underlined part. If the underlined
            part is correct, circle the word *correct.* If it is wrong, circle the wrong part
            and write the correct form above it.

correct	wrong	1. What time <u>does first show</u> start?
correct	wrong	2. My favorite food <u>is cheese</u> with crackers.
correct	wrong	3. Los Angeles, San Francisco, and Sacramento are <u>in same</u> state.
correct	wrong	4. <u>The United Nations</u> has its main office in New York City.
correct	wrong	5. The longest river in the United States is <u>the</u> Mississippi.
correct	wrong	6. In Canada, <u>the English and the French</u> are official languages.
correct	wrong	7. When I went to the store yesterday, I <u>bought new</u> blue shirt.
correct	wrong	8. The flight to Paris departs from <u>the</u> gate seven.

Unit 3

*Be + Going to +*VERB

1. affirmative   3. *yes-no* questions   5. discrimination with other tenses
2. negative   4. short answers

Discover Grammar

1. Write one of the six time expressions in the blank. Use each time expression one time.

yesterday	5 days ago	right now
tomorrow	every day	next week

   (a) He is playing tennis with Joe _____.

   (b) I studied vocabulary _____.

   (c) I eat a big breakfast _____.

   (d) She called me _____.

   (e) I'm going to call you _____.

   (f) Are you going to go to Boston _____?

2. Look at the verbs in each sentence. Four of the sentences have verb tenses that we studied in this book. Two of the sentences have a verb form that we did not study. What is the new form?

   _____

3. Question: When do we use *be + going to?*

   _____

   [Check p. 37 for the answer to this question.]

Be Going to + VERB

Affirmative Statements

I'**m going to call** Susan tomorrow.
You'**re going to visit** Bob next week.
He'**s going to read** a book next month.
It'**s going to rain** tomorrow.
We'**re going to paint** the house in May.
They'**re going to have** a great time.

Negative Statements

I'**m not going to call** Jenny tonight.
You'**re not going to be** late again.
He **isn't going to take** a trip in two days.★
It **isn't going to rain** tomorrow night.
We **aren't going to paint** the house in June.
They'**re not going to cook** spaghetti tonight.

Yes-No Questions and Short Answers

A: **Are you and Jim going to eat** together?

B: Yes, we **are**.

A: **Are we going to have** a test tomorrow?

B: No, we **aren't**.

A: Wow! **Are you going to go** to Tahiti?

B: Yes, I **am**. I'm going to be there a week.

A: **Is it going to snow** tonight?

B: No, it **isn't**. It's going to rain.

★ **In** + **TIME** is the opposite of **TIME** + **ago.** We use **in** + **TIME** for actions in the future.

examples: I was in New York two weeks ago. I'm going to be in Paris in three days.

                He moved here one month ago. He's going to buy a house in two weeks.

SUBJECT + *Be* + *Going to* + VERB

For actions or events in the future, we can use **SUBJECT** + **be** + **going to** + **VERB**.

I'm going to go	I'm going to be	I'm going to study	I'm going to make
you're going to go	you're going to be	you're going to study	you're going to make
he's going to go	he's going to be	he's going to study	he's going to make
she's going to go	she's going to be	she's going to study	she's going to make
it's going to go	it's going to be	★	it's going to make
we're going to go	we're going to be	we're going to study	we're going to make
they're going to go	they're going to be	they're going to study	they're going to make

★"It's going to study" doesn't have any meaning. The grammar is possible, but a thing (= it) cannot study.

CAREFUL! Watch out for these common mistakes.

1. Don't forget to use **be**.

   wrong: Laura going to cook scrambled eggs for breakfast tomorrow.

   correct: Laura's going to cook scrambled eggs for breakfast tomorrow.

   wrong: I going to study with Mike and Kim tonight.

   correct: I am going to study with Mike and Kim tonight.

2. Don't forget the word **to**. It's a small word, but it is very important.

   wrong: The teacher is going be absent tomorrow.

   correct: The teacher is going to be absent tomorrow.

   wrong: Maureen is going do the dishes after dinner.

   correct: Maureen is going to do the dishes after dinner.

3. Don't use **s** or **ed** or **ing** with the verb after **to.**

   wrong: He's going to studies with me.

   correct: He's going to study with me.

   wrong: I'm going to walked to school tomorrow morning.

   correct: I'm going to walk to school tomorrow morning.

   wrong: Virginia is going to driving her car to Miami.

   correct: Virginia is going to drive her car to Miami.

Exercise 1.   Fill in the blanks with the correct forms of *work*. Follow the examples.

VERB

1. I _work_ all of the time.

2. You _____ every day.

3. He _____ most of the time.

4. She _____ every morning.

5. It _____ most of the time.

6. We _____ some of the time.

7. They _____ every day.

VERB + *ed*

8. I _worked_ yesterday.

9. You _____ last night.

10. He _____ a year ago.

11. She _____ last Monday.

12. It _____ yesterday.

13. We _____ in 1974.

14. They _____ last summer.

***be + going to* + VERB**

15. I _am going to work_ next week.

16. You _____ tomorrow.

17. He _____ in five minutes.

18. She _____ next year.

19. It _____ tomorrow.

20. We _____ next Monday.

21. They _____ next summer.

Exercise 2.   Read the time expression and then write the correct form of the verb. Follow the example.

Every Day	*Tomorrow*

1. I study French.   I am going to study French.

2. She reads the newspaper.   _____

3. They do homework.   _____

Now	*Tomorrow*

4. He is eating salad.   _____

5. We are going to the zoo.   _____

6. I am studying.   _____

Yesterday	*Tomorrow*

7. She studied grammar.   _____

8. He worked at the store.   _____

9. They visited Jim.   _____

Now	*Next Week*

10. He is going to the bank.   _____

11. We are playing tennis.   _____

12. I am reading an interesting book.   _____

Yesterday	*In an Hour*

13. She called her mother.   _____

14. He watched a movie on TV.   _____

15. They washed their car.   _____

Exercise 3.   Read the question and then write a *no* answer to the question. In your answer, write a statement using *tomorrow, next week, in ten minutes,* or some other future expression. Follow the example.

example: Did you study last night?
 No, I'm going to study tonight.

1. Did you cook spaghetti this week?

   _____

2. Did Lisa call you last night?

   _____

3. Did you do the homework?

   _____

4. Were you on time for work this morning?

   _____

5. Did Kathleen and Sue go to New York yesterday?

   _____

6. Did you buy a present for Keith?

   _____

Answers to DISCOVER GRAMMAR from page 33:

1. a. right now   b. yesterday (or 5 days ago)   c. every day   d. 5 days ago (or yesterday)
   e. tomorrow (or next week)   f. next week (or tomorrow)
2. *be* + *going to* + VERB
3. for future actions

Exercise 4.   Write a *yes-no* question and give a short answer. Then write a *wh*-question and give a short answer. (*Hint:* Look at the word in italics.) Follow the example.

example: Karen is going to write *a letter to the president.*

(yes-no)   Is Karen going to write a letter to the president?

Yes, she is.

(wh)   What is Karen going to write?

A letter to the president.

1. Paul is going to play tennis *this weekend.*

    (y-n) _____

    _____

    (wh) _____

    _____

2. Tina is going to fly *to New York* in an hour.

    (y-n) _____

    _____

    (wh) _____

    _____

3. The girls are going to watch a movie *tonight.*

    (y-n) _____

    _____

    (wh) _____

    _____

4. *Victor* is going to work for eleven hours tomorrow.

    (y-n) _____

    _____

    (wh) _____

    _____

5. Laura is going to study tonight. *She has a big test tomorrow.*

    (y-n) _____

    _____

(wh) _____

_____

Exercise 5.   Verb Discrimination: Present, Past, Present Progressive, Future.
Underline the correct form of the verb. Follow the example.

example: The boys (<u>are going to work</u>, are working, worked, work)
here tomorrow.

1. The boy (is going to play, is playing, played, plays) tennis last week.

2. Mark and Joe (are going to study, are studying, studied, study) vocabulary next week.

3. We (are going to be, are being, were, are) on the plane in one hour from now.

4. Susan (is going to attend, is attending, attends, attend) class every day.

5. They (are going to need, are needing, needed, need) a camera right now.

6. John, Mike, and Susan (are going to listen, are listening, listened,
   listen) to the radio now.

7. I (am going to assist, am assisting, assisted, assist) the doctor yesterday.

8. It (is going to rain, is raining, rained, rains) right now.

9. You and John (are going to do, are doing, did, do) the homework
   last night.

10. They usually (are going to visit, are visiting, visits, visit) Mrs. Jones on Monday.

CHALLENGE   This is similar to number 5 above. Another student in your class
always says, "I'm needing some help." Is this correct? You are the teacher now. Can you
explain the problem here?

Note to advanced students: Although present progressive is used for now or right now, it is
also correct to use present progressive for future action if you name the time. For example,
"Mark and Joe are studying vocabulary next week" and "We're having a test tomorrow"
are good sentences.

Exercise 6.   Verb Discrimination: Present, Past, Present Progressive, Future.
Write the correct form of the verb on the line. Follow the example.

example: play They __are playing__ tennis now.
We __played__ tennis yesterday.
He __is going to play__ tennis tomorrow.
She __plays__ tennis every day.

study

   1. She _____ grammar now.

   2. They _____ vocabulary last night.

   3. He always _____ spelling.

   4. I _____ grammar tomorrow.

do

   5. You _____ the homework last night.

   6. I _____ the exercises every day.

   7. We _____ lesson 5 right now.

   8. She _____ the questions tomorrow.

need

   9. We _____ some help last week.

 10. We _____ a car next week.

 11. I always _____ more money.

 12. I _____ money right now.

be

 13. I _____ a businessman.

 14. I _____ in Venezuela last year.

 15. I _____ in France next month.

 16. I _____ in Canada now.

work (use *you* in the questions)

 17. _____ every day?

 18. _____ in a nice office now?

 19. _____ in Korea last year?

 20. _____ there next month?

rain (use *it* in the questions)

 21. _____ tomorrow?

 22. _____ yesterday?

 23. _____ every day in August?

 24. _____ right now?

Speaking Activity

Exercise 7.   Speaking: Question Game

Step 1.   There are six actions and six future times below. Use them to write your schedule for tomorrow.

Step 2.   After you finish writing, work with a partner. Take turns asking questions to try to guess your partner's schedule. If the answer to a question is YES, then that person can continue asking. If the answer is NO, the turn passes to the other student. The first partner to finish is the winner!

Action		*Time*	
go to the library	make soup	at 10 A.M. tomorrow	at 5 P.M. tomorrow
do the dishes	wash clothes	at 8 P.M. tomorrow night	at 2 P.M. tomorrow
watch a movie on TV	call Paula	at noon tomorrow	at 4 P.M. tomorrow

Write your schedule.

Action   *Time*

I'm going to _____   _____.

I'm going to _____   _____.

I'm going to _____   _____.

I'm going to _____   _____.

I'm going to _____   _____.

I'm going to _____   _____.

Your partner's schedule.

Action   *Time*

action: _____   time: _____

action: _____   time: _____

action: _____   time: _____

action: _____   time: _____

action: _____   time: _____

action: _____   time: _____

Exercise 8.   Multiple Choice. Circle the letter of the correct answer.

1. "_____ work every day?"

   "No, I work from Tuesday to Saturday. I don't work on Sunday and Monday."

   (A) Are you going to   (C) Do you

   (B) Are you   (D) Did you

2. "Are you busy tomorrow?"

   "No, I _____ anything."

   (A) am not do   (C) am not going to do

   (B) do not do   (D) did not do

3. We _____ play tennis next week.

   (A) don't going to   (C) don't going

   (B) aren't going to   (D) aren't going

4. "Are you going to eat dinner soon?"

   "Yes, _____."

   (A) you're   (C) we're

   (B) you are   (D) we are

5. "_____ study for the test?"

   "No, I'm going to study for the test tonight."

   (A) Did you   (C) Were you

   (B) Are you going to   (D) Are you

6. Sometimes I eat a big breakfast, but tomorrow morning I'm _____ do that.

   (A) not going to   (C) not going

   (B) don't to   (D) don't

7. "It's so hot in here!"

   "Yes, it is. I _____ turn on the air conditioner."

   (A) am going to   (C) going to

   (B) am going   (D) be going

8. "You look sick. Are you feeling OK?

   "No, I'm not. _____ to the doctor's office."

   (A) You're going to go   (C) You're go to going

   (B) I'm going to going   (D) I'm going to go

Exercise 9.   Review Test

Part 1. Fill in the blanks with any word or words that make sense.

1. Tomorrow I'm _____ to drive to Miami.

2. Yesterday I _____ English with my friend because we had a big test today.

3. I have a meeting with Mr. Smith in 10 minutes. We _____ to talk about new business.

4. *Teacher:*   Don't forget. There is a test next week.

   Student: Is the test going _____ hard?

5. *Mary:*   The weather today is so bad. It's _____ so hard! And I don't have an umbrella.

   John: Yes, it's terrible. And tomorrow it _____ again!

6. *Mary:*   What time _____ to sleep at night?

   John: I usually go to sleep around 11 P.M. What about you?

7. I am very tired, so I'm not _____ go to the party tonight.

Part 2. Read each sentence carefully. Look at the underlined part. If the underlined part is correct, circle the word *correct*. If it is wrong, circle the wrong part and write the correct form above.

correct   wrong   1. John, Sue, and I <u>are going to watch</u> TV last night.

correct   wrong   2. Those shirts <u>are going to be</u> on sale next week.

correct   wrong   3. I was late for work today, but tomorrow I'm <u>going be</u> on time for work.

correct   wrong   4. She always eats eggs for breakfast, but <u>tomorrow she's going to eats</u> bread.

correct   wrong   5. We're going <u>to go</u> to France next year, but they're going there this week.

correct   wrong   6. <u>Do Mike and John going</u> to play tennis tomorrow?

correct   wrong   7. Why are they going to <u>writing</u> their homework with a red pen?

correct   wrong   8. <u>Laura going</u> to make salad, and I'm going to make cheese sandwiches.

Unit 4

Irregular Past Tense

1. affirmative 2. negative 3. questions

Did you catch any fish this morning?

Yes, I caught five fish.

List of Irregular Past Tense Verbs

You know that most verbs form the past tense with **ed: learned, studied, played**.
However, there are some verbs in English that do not use **ed.** The past tense for these
verbs is different. The number of these verbs is very small (about 100), but these verbs are
used very frequently. Look at these irregular past forms.

Present	*Past*	*Present*	*Past*	*Present*	*Past*
become	became	do	did	go	went
begin	began	draw	drew	grow	grew
bite	bit	drink	drank	hang	hung
blow	blew	drive	drove	have	had
break	broke	eat	ate	hear	heard
bring	brought	fall	fell	hide	hid
build	built	feel	felt	hold	held
buy	bought	fight	fought	hurt	hurt
catch	caught	find	found	keep	kept
choose	chose	fly	flew	know	knew
come	came	forget	forgot	lead	led
cost	cost	get	got	leave	left
cut	cut	give	gave	lend	lent

Present	Past	Present	Past	Present	Past
let	let	sell	sold	stick	stuck
lie★	lay	send	sent	swim	swam
lose	lost	set	set	take	took
make	made	shoot	shot	teach	taught
mean	meant	shut	shut	tear	tore
meet	met	sing	sang	tell	told
put	put	sit	sat	think	thought
read	read	sleep	slept	throw	threw
ride	rode	speak	spoke	understand	understood
ring	rang	spend	spent	wake	woke
run	ran	spread	spread	wear	wore
say	said	stand	stood	win	won
see	saw	steal	stole	write	wrote

★lie = lie down (recline); not tell the truth = lie, lied

Negative

I **went** to the park.	I **didn't go** to the store.
You **went** to Miami.	You **did not go** to New York.
He **went** to school.	He **didn't go** to the bank.
She **went** to France.	She **didn't go** to Italy.
The plane **went** to Mexico.	It **didn't go** to Colombia.
We **went** to the store.	We **did not go** home.
They **went** to China.	They **didn't go** to Japan.

Negative: **SUBJECT + did not (didn't) + SIMPLE VERB**

Questions

I **sat** in the wrong chair.	**Did** I **sit** in the wrong chair?
You **ate** all the cheese.	**Did** you **eat** all the cheese?
He **spoke** to Dr. Karl.	**Did** he **speak** to Dr. Karl?
She **ran** to the bank.	**Did** she **run** to the bank?
It **took** one hour to do the work.	**Did** it **take** one hour to do the work?
We **sang** that song two times.	**Did** we **sing** that song two times?
They **brought** a lot of cassettes.	**Did** they **bring** a lot of cassettes?

Question: **did + SUBJECT + SIMPLE VERB**

CAREFUL! Watch out for these common mistakes.

1. Do not use **ed** with irregular verbs.

    wrong: My sister goed to England last year.
    correct: My sister went to England last year.

    wrong: He weared a dark blue suit to the party last night.
    correct: He wore a dark blue suit to the party last night.

2. Do not use the irregular past tense form with **did** in the question. **Did** is past, and you only need a past tense form in one place in the verb.

    wrong: Did you rode your bike to school? (= 2 past tense words)
    correct: Did you ride your bike to school?

    wrong: Did they drank all the juice? (= 2 past tense words)
    correct: Did they drink all the juice?

3. Do not use the irregular past tense form in a negative. **Didn't (did not)** is past, and you only need a past tense form in one place in the verb.

    wrong: She didn't understood the lesson. (= 2 past tense words)
    correct: She didn't understand the lesson.

    wrong: Sammy did not knew the answer. (= 2 past tense words)
    correct: Sammy did not know the answer.

Exercise 1. Write the present tense of the verb on the line. Follow the examples.

Present	Past		Present	Past		Present	Past
1. _go_	went	12.		sold	23.		grew
2. _bring_	brought	13.		sang	24.		heard
3.	shut	14.		cut	25.		lent
4.	stole	15.		swam	26.		lost
5.	drove	16.		made	27.		fell
6.	told	17.		caught	28.		kept
7.	chose	18.		cost	29.		left
8.	sent	19.		had	30.		threw
9.	flew	20.		woke	31.		wore
10.	got	21.		said	32.		saw
11.	wrote	22.		gave	33.		ate

Exercise 2.   Write the past tense of the verb on the line. Follow the examples.

examples: come __came__   buy __bought__

1. drink	_____	11. break	_____
2. give	_____	12. eat	_____
3. become	_____	13. know	_____
4. read	_____	14. keep	_____
5. begin	_____	15. speak	_____
6. get	_____	16. forget	_____
7. see	_____	17. tear	_____
8. wear	_____	18. come	_____
9. take	_____	19. write	_____
10. sit	_____	20. choose	_____

Exercise 3.   Write the past tense of the verb on the line. Follow the examples.

examples: get __got__   think __thought__

1. break	_____	11. know	_____
2. bring	_____	12. mean	_____
3. eat	_____	13. wear	_____
4. do	_____	14. are	_____
5. wake	_____	15. buy	_____
6. cut	_____	16. choose	_____
7. feel	_____	17. go	_____
8. begin	_____	18. ride	_____
9. find	_____	19. send	_____
10. leave	_____	20. stick	_____

Exercise 4. Make a test for a classmate. What are twenty of the most difficult verbs? Write the present tense forms of twenty verbs on the left lines. Then give your book to a classmate. The classmate should write the correct past tense forms. Check your partner's answers.

Present	*Past*		*Present*	*Past*
1. _____	_____		11. _____	_____
2. _____	_____		12. _____	_____
3. _____	_____		13. _____	_____
4. _____	_____		14. _____	_____
5. _____	_____		15. _____	_____
6. _____	_____		16. _____	_____
7. _____	_____		17. _____	_____
8. _____	_____		18. _____	_____
9. _____	_____		19. _____	_____
10. _____	_____		20. _____	_____

Exercise 5. Read the sentence carefully and then underline the correct verb form. Some sentences are present time, and some sentences are past time. Follow the examples.

examples: Every day I (take, took) the bus to work. It's not expensive.
I (write, wrote) six letters last night.

1. Yesterday I (go, went) to the doctor's office because I (feel, felt) sick.

2. Mr. Jones usually (does, did) the dishes after dinner.

3. I (find, found) the woman's wallet. She was so happy. She (gives, gave) me $100.

4. I (know, knew) only 6 of the answers on the last test.

5. Mark (sees, saw) very well because he has new glasses.

6. I (sit, sat) in the front of the class because I want to see the blackboard well.

7. My father (writes, wrote) with his left hand. He is the only left-handed person in my family.

8. In 1901, Guglielmo Marconi (sends, sent) the first transatlantic message from Europe to Newfoundland, Canada.

9. Does anyone know how many years Muhammad Ali (holds, held) the title of World Champion?

10. Bill (makes, made) tea for us. We drank it, and then we talked about school.

11. I was surprised because the cat (catches, caught) the ball with its two front paws.

12. Mr. Bryan (teaches, taught) at Hillsboro High School now. He (teaches, taught) in New York City from 1992 to 1995.

Exercise 6. Write the correct form of the verb on the chart. Follow the examples.

	Present Statement	Present Negative	Past Statement	Past Negative	Present Question	Past Question
1.	he goes	he doesn't go	he went	he didn't go	Does he go	Did he go
2.	they catch				Do they catch	
3.			we had			
4.				she didn't get		
5.		I don't wake				
6.					Do you sell	
7.						Did you lose
8.	it takes					
9.			he spoke			
10.					Do I keep	
11.				he didn't steal		
12.				she didn't cut		
13.		we don't know				
14.						Did they tear

Exercise 7.   Answer these questions with complete sentences. Follow the examples.

1. Did John eat an apple? (yes)   <u>Yes, he ate an apple.</u>

2. Did Mark buy a new shirt? (no)   <u>No, he didn't buy a new shirt.</u>

3. Did she begin the work? (no)   _____

4. Did you see that movie? (yes)   _____

5. Did you forget my book? (no)   _____

6. Did the phone ring five times? (no) _____

7. Did she put the shoes in the closet? (yes) _____

8. Did they break the glass? (yes)   _____

CHALLENGE   A student says the answer for 3 is *No, she didn't began the work.*
Another student says the answer is *No, she doesn't began the work.* You are the teacher now.
Which student is correct? Explain your answer.

Exercise 8.   Write the correct form of the verb on the line. Follow the example.

example: (meet) I <u>met</u> him yesterday.

1. (give)   She _____ me a check a few minutes ago.

2. (come)   Did you _____ late?

3. (take)   I _____ my medicine over an

           hour ago.

4   (forget)   He didn't _____ the telephone

           number.

5. (break)   Who _____ the window?

6. (be)   Mark and I _____ in Saudi Arabia for one year.

7. (begin)   The class _____ ten minutes ago.

8. (give)   He didn't _____ me the money yesterday.

9. (eat)   We _____ steak last night.

10. (get)   Martha _____ sick yesterday.

Exercise 9.   Write a complete answer to the question. Use the italicized word as the answer. Follow the example.

example: Did he send *a box* or an envelope?   <u>He sent a box.</u>

1. Did they eat cake or *steak*? _____

2. Did I tell you *yes* or no? _____

3. Did Robert make coffee or *tea*? _____

4. Did you sleep *six hours* or seven hours? _____

5. Did she bring one book or *two books*? _____

6. Did she buy that house *in 1985* or 1987? _____

7. Did he cut his left hand or *his right hand*? _____

8. Did you hear the news *this morning* or last night? _____

9. Did you choose *answer A* or answer B? _____

10. Did Luke get up at six or *at seven*? _____

Speaking Activity

Exercise 10.   Speaking Activity. What did you do yesterday?

Step 1.   What did you do yesterday? There are twelve activities below. Put a check mark (√) by any five of the activities. Student A works in the left column. Student B works in the right column.

Step 2.   Next, work with a partner. Do NOT show your book to your partner. Take turns asking each other questions. Say "yesterday" in every question. If the answer is YES, then you continue. If the answer is NO, then it is your partner's turn. *Use complete sentences in your answers.*

examples: A: Did you come to class late yesterday?
            B: No, I didn't come to class late.

(The answer is NO, so it is B's turn.)

            B: Did you eat salad yesterday?
            A: Yes, I ate salad yesterday.

(The answer is YES, so B asks again.)

The winner is the first student to guess all five of the activities that the other student did yesterday.

Student A	Student B
___ wake up at 7 A.M.	___ wake up at 8 A.M.
___ take a shower in the morning	___ take a bath in the morning
___ eat toast for breakfast	___ eat eggs for breakfast
___ ride your bike to school	___ drive your car to school
___ run in the afternoon	___ run in the evening
___ write a letter to your friend	___ speak to your teacher
___ draw any pictures	___ buy a sandwich
___ find any money in the street	___ read a newspaper
___ have a headache	___ drink apple juice
___ spend more than $5	___ spend more than $10
___ lose your watch	___ get a letter from your friend
___ see a cat	___ come to class late

Speaking Activity

Exercise 11.   Speaking Activity. Who did what? There are two groups of names and actions. Student A should do one group, and student B should do the other group. In each group, there are seven people's names and seven actions.

Step 1.   Work in your area only (A or B). Draw a line to connect the seven subjects and seven actions. Mix up the lines. You will make seven new sentences. On the line (_____), write the past tense form. For example, if student A draws a line from "Sammy" to "eat fish for dinner," then the new sentence in the past tense is "Sammy ate fish for dinner." Remember we are practicing past tense of irregular verbs.

Step 2.   Now work with a partner. You will ask questions about your partner's sentences in order to guess his or her seven sentences. Student A will ask about B's lines, and student B will ask about A's lines. For example, student A can ask, "Did Susan drive to Miami?" If student B has a line now from "Susan" to "drive to Miami," then B says, "Yes, Susan drove to Miami. That's correct." And it is still student A's turn to ask another question. If student B does not have a line from "Susan" to "drive to Miami," then B says, "No, Susan didn't drive to Miami. That's not correct." And it is student B's turn to ask a question. The winner is the first student to guess all seven of his or her partner's lines (sentences).

Student A

Sammy _____ (go) to the park

Maria _____ (wake) up at 6 A.M.

Paul _____ (eat) fish for dinner

Joe and Sue _____ (find) a ten-dollar bill in the street

Mr. Mills _____ (sing) some songs

Chang _____ (fly) to Paris last year

Julie _____ (buy) some fried chicken

Student B

Jonathan _____ (make) a chocolate cake

Susan _____ (get) up at 7 A.M.

Kirk _____ (drive) to Miami

Tim and Bob _____ (spend) one hundred dollars on shoes

Mrs. Wilson _____ (understand) the math lesson

Pierre _____ (know) all the answers on the test

Mohamad _____ (have) a car accident

Speaking Activity

Exercise 12.   Speaking Activity. The Shopping Bag Game. Work with a partner. Each partner chooses one of these sixteen shopping bags. Take turns asking *yes-no* questions to find out which bag is your partner's bag. If student B's answer is YES, student A may continue asking questions. If the answer is NO, then student B asks questions. The first student to guess the price of his or her partner's shopping bag is the winner. Use "Did you buy _____?" and "Yes, I bought _____" or "No, I didn't buy _____" in your conversations.

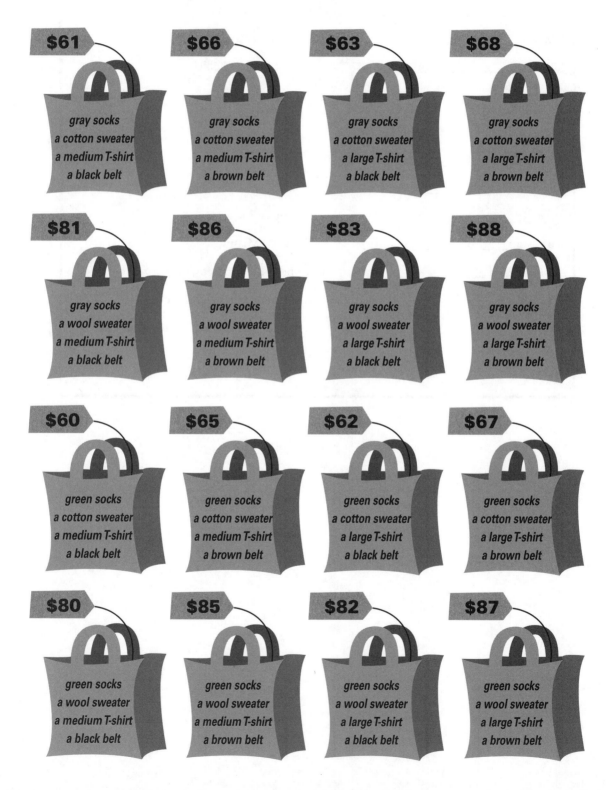

$61
gray socks
a cotton sweater
a medium T-shirt
a black belt

$66
gray socks
a cotton sweater
a medium T-shirt
a brown belt

$63
gray socks
a cotton sweater
a large T-shirt
a black belt

$68
gray socks
a cotton sweater
a large T-shirt
a brown belt

$81
gray socks
a wool sweater
a medium T-shirt
a black belt

$86
gray socks
a wool sweater
a medium T-shirt
a brown belt

$83
gray socks
a wool sweater
a large T-shirt
a black belt

$88
gray socks
a wool sweater
a large T-shirt
a brown belt

$60
green socks
a cotton sweater
a medium T-shirt
a black belt

$65
green socks
a cotton sweater
a medium T-shirt
a brown belt

$62
green socks
a cotton sweater
a large T-shirt
a black belt

$67
green socks
a cotton sweater
a large T-shirt
a brown belt

$80
green socks
a wool sweater
a medium T-shirt
a black belt

$85
green socks
a wool sweater
a medium T-shirt
a brown belt

$82
green socks
a wool sweater
a large T-shirt
a black belt

$87
green socks
a wool sweater
a large T-shirt
a brown belt

Exercise 13.   Multiple Choice. Circle the letter of the correct answer.

1. "Where are the books?"

   "I _____ them on the desk near the door."

   (A) putting   (C) put

   (B) putted   (D) did put

2. "What time did he start the work?"

   "He _____ at about 7 P.M."

   (A) begin   (C) begins

   (B) began   (D) beginned

3. "You look terrible. What's wrong?"

   "I have a cold. I _____ to the doctor because it's not so bad."

   (A) goed   (C) didn't go

   (B) went   (D) don't went

4. "_____ to Miami?"

   "Yes, we took Northwest Airlines."

   (A) Do you fly   (C) Did you fly

   (B) Did you flew   (D) Do you flew

5. "Do you know Teresa?"

   "Yes, of course. I _____ her at a dinner party at John's house."

   (A) met   (C) meeted

   (B) meeting   (D) did met

6. "Mrs. Chan was absent today."

   "Oh, really? Did Mrs. Henry _____ in her place?"

   (A) teach   (C) taught

   (B) taucht   (D) teached

7. "Did you find your keys?"

   "Yes, I _____. They were on the floor near the sofa."

   (A) did   (C) found

   (B) do   (D) find

8. "Where is your homework?"

   "I _____ it."

   (A) don't   (C) didn't

   (B) don't do   (D) didn't do

Exercise 14.   Review Test

Part 1. Read these sentences. Underline the correct verb form.

1. I didn't (choose, choosed, chose, choosing) the red shirt.

2. She (make, makes, made, making) a big tuna fish sandwich a

     few minutes ago.

3. I asked the teacher a question because I (don't understand,

     don't understood, didn't understand, didn't understood) the lesson.

4. What did you (drink, drinking, drinked, dranked) for breakfast?

5. That shirt is very nice! How much did it (cost, costed, costing) you?★

★ *Cultural Note:* It is often considered rude to ask people the cost of something. Sometimes it is OK if the
    two people know each other very well.

Part 2. Read this short paragraph. Fill in each blank with the correct form of a verb.

      Yesterday was a very hectic day for me. I usually wake up at 6 A.M., but yesterday I

_____ up late. I _____ a shower and then I _____ dressed. I didn't have

time for breakfast, so I _____ breakfast. Of course I was hungry all day because of

this. I usually take the bus to work. But yesterday I was late, so I _____ my own car.

It's faster than taking the bus because the bus makes many stops.

Part 3.   Read each sentence carefully. Look at the underlined part. If the under-
            lined part is correct, circle the word *correct*. If it is wrong, circle the wrong
            part and write the correct form above.

correct   wrong   1. She <u>isn't go</u> to England in 1975.

correct   wrong   2. <u>Do you eat</u> breakfast at your friend's house yesterday?

correct   wrong   3. I <u>put</u> my shoes in the closet when I got home.

correct   wrong   4. <u>Did you understand</u> yesterday's class?

correct   wrong   5. John didn't have any money, so Maria <u>lent</u> him a few dollars.

correct   wrong   6. He <u>didn't gave</u> me his telephone number.

correct   wrong   7. Last night I <u>readed</u> all the homework.

correct   wrong   8. Joe was lucky. He <u>founded</u> $10 in the street.

Unit 5

How Questions

1. *how many* vs. *how much*
2. *how far*
3. *how* + **ADJECTIVE** (*long, big, tall, expensive, etc.*)
4. *how old*
5. *how often*

How long is your reading class?

It's 50 minutes long.

How Questions

Question	Answer	Explanation
How many books do you have?	8	**How many** = things you can count
How much sugar is in the bag?	2 pounds	**How much** = things you can't count
How far is your house from here?	2 miles	**How far** is for distance.
How long is a soccer field?	200 meters	**How long** = length, distance
How long is this class?	50 minutes	**How long** = time
How big is your house?	1,200 square feet	
How tall is your father?	6 feet	
How expensive was that watch?	It was $200.	**How + ADJECTIVE** = the degree of ___
How angry was Victor?	He was furious!	
How high is that mountain?	It's 6,000 feet.	
How old was Washington when he became president?	I don't know.	**How old** = age
How often do you play soccer?	Every day	**How often** = frequency

(See p. 69 for more on **how often**.)

CAREFUL! Watch out for these common mistakes.

1. Do not use **what** in place of **how**.
   wrong: What big is your house?
   correct: How big is your house?

2. Do not use **how long** in place of **how tall**.
   wrong: How long is Susan?
   correct: How tall is Susan?

3. Do not forget to use question word order.
   wrong: How old your brother is?
   correct: How old is your brother?

4. Remember that **how many** is for count nouns and **how much** is for noncount nouns. Do not mix them up.
   wrong: How much books do you need?
   correct: How many books do you need?

Exercise 1.   Underline the correct question words. Follow the example.

example: Q: How (much, <u>long</u>, tall) is the Mississippi River?
               A: About 2,340 miles.

1. Q: How (many, big, old) is your family?

   A: I have 4 brothers but no sisters.

2. Q: How (much, long, tall) does she weigh?

   A: 110 pounds.

3. Q: How (much, long, tall) did you work there?

   A: Almost 10 years.

4. Q: How (sad, long, angry) was your father?

   A: He shouted at me and his face turned red.

5. Q: How (many, expensive, much) did

   those pants cost you?

   A: They were on sale. Only $23.99.

6. Q: How (much, long, tall) is Mr. Lim?

   A: He's 6'2".★

7. Q: How (much, long, tall) was he sick?

   A: For 2 weeks.

8. Q: How (much, long, tall) is the pool?

   A: 40 feet.

9. Q: How (many, tall, long) is she?

   A: I think she's about 5'7".

10. Q: How (much, long, many) people

    came to the party?

    A: Only about a dozen or so.

★ 6'2" What does this mean? The first number is the person's height in feet. It is marked with one line ('), so 5' means five feet. The second number is inches. It is marked with two small lines ("), so 4" means four inches. 6'2" means six feet, two inches tall. This system is only used for how tall someone (or something) is. Twelve inches is equal to one foot (12" = 1').

Exercise 2. Fill in the blanks with the correct question words. Follow the example.

example: Q: ___How big___ is your car?
A: It can hold five people fine.

1. Q: _____ is your family?

A: I have 2 brothers and 1 sister.

2. Q: _____ does he weigh?

A: 180 pounds.

3. Q: _____ were you sick?

A: Two days.

4. Q: _____ is Mike's house from here?

A: Six miles.

5. Q: _____ was your father?

A: He was very sick. He almost died.

6. Q: _____ is your father?

A: He's 6'2".

7. Q: _____ did you study there?

A: For three years.

8. Q: _____ is your house from here?

A: Not far. It's next to the park.

9. Q: _____ did that shirt cost you?

A: $17.50.

10. Q: _____ people were at the party?

A: Oh, between 30 and 40, I think.

Exercise 3. Write a *how* question for these sentences. (*Hint:* The words in italics can help you write the correct question.) Follow the example.

example: Ben studies *for an hour* every day.
___How long does Ben study every day?___

1. Frank and Mark work in the garden *for two hours* every Saturday.

_____

2. Victor drives 30 miles to his office *every day*.

_____

3. Victor drives *30* miles to his office every day.

_____

4. Victor drives *30 miles* to his office every day.

_____

5. Laura is *5'6"* tall.

_____

6. Laura weighs *135 pounds*.

_____

7. Laura is *38 years* old.

_____

8. Tina's math class is *50 minutes* long.

_____

CHALLENGE A student says the answer for 7 is *What is Laura's age?* instead of *How old is Laura?* Both of these are correct English questions. What is the difference between using a *what* question and a *how* question? Other examples are *How tall are you?* vs. *What is your height?* or *How long is that string?* vs. *What is the length of that string?*

Speaking Activity

Exercise 4a. Speaking Activity: Flight Schedule—Student A

Step 1. Work with a partner. Student A works here and on page 61; student B works on page 62. The chart has information about Pan World Airlines daily flights. However, some of the information is missing. Take turns asking your partner questions about the missing information. First, make five practice questions about the flight from New York to Paris. You have all the information for this flight, but this is just practice. Check your five questions with someone. Make sure you understand how to make these questions correctly before you start step 2.

5 practice questions:

1. _____

2. _____

3. _____

4. _____

5. _____

Step 2. Work with your partner. The chart below has information about some flights. Some of the information is not here. Take turns asking each other questions to get the information that you need to complete the chart.

Information for Pan World Airlines Daily Flights					
From — To —	*Distance (miles)*	*Duration (hours:min)*	*Ticket Price*	*No. of Stops*	*Pilot's Age on Today's Flight*
New York to Paris	3,635	7:15	$ 600	0	38
Miami to Hong Kong		18:56	$ 1,220		52
Vancouver to Rio de Janeiro					
Ottawa to Kuwait City	6,421		$ 1,447	2	46
Cairo to London	2,196	5:05		1	

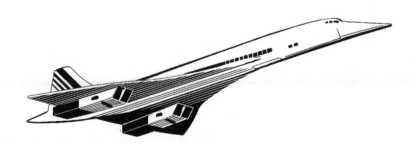

Speaking Activity

Exercise 4b.   Speaking Activity: Flight Schedule—Student B

Step 1. Work with a partner. Student B works here; student A works on pages 60 and 61. The chart has information about Pan World Airlines daily flights. However, some of the information is missing. Take turns asking your partner questions about the missing information. First, make five practice questions about the flight from New York to Paris. You have all the information for this flight, but this is just practice. Check your five questions with someone. Make sure you understand how to make these questions correctly before you start step 2.

5 practice questions: 1. _____

2. _____

3. _____

4. _____

5. _____

Step 2. Work with your partner. The chart below has information about some flights. Some of the information is not here. Take turns asking each other questions to get the information that you need to complete the chart.

Information for Pan World Airlines Daily Flights					
From — To —	*Distance (miles)*	*Duration (hours:min)*	*Ticket Price*	*No. of Stops*	*Pilot's Age on Today's Flight*
New York to Paris	3,635	7:15	$ 600	0	38
Miami to Hong Kong	8,984			2	
Vancouver to Rio de Janeiro	6,955	17:20	$ 720	1	47
Ottawa to Kuwait City		14:10			
Cairo to London			$ 550		29

Exercise 5.   Multiple Choice. Circle the letter of the correct answer.

1. "How _____ is the library from here?"

    "I think it's about 2 miles."

    (A) long   (C) far

    (B) much   (D) busy

2. "How _____ did Jim and Sam work together?"

    "Only about 2 months. Then Sam changed to a different company."

    (A) long   (C) much

    (B) many   (D) old

3. "How _____ is that book?"

    "It has 427 pages! I'm never going to finish it!"

    (A) heavy   (C) many

    (B) far   (D) long

4. "How _____ was the teacher when you came late?"

    "Her face was as red as blood!"

    (A) tall   (C) angry

    (B) old   (D) pretty

5. "How _____?"

    "I'm not very sure, but he's taller than I am."

    (A) tall is William   (C) tall William is

    (B) William is tall   (D) William tall is

6. "_____ people work in your office with you?"

    (A) What number of   (C) What many

    (B) How number of   (D) How many

7. "How much _____?"

    (A) he weighs   (C) does he weigh

    (B) weighs he   (D) is he weigh

8. "How _____ pounds are in a kilo?"

    "2.2."

    (A) much   (C) heavy

    (B) many   (D) far

Exercise 6.   Review Test

Part 1.   Fill in the blanks with the correct words to complete these questions.

1. *A:* How _____ is that mountain?

    B: 4,250 feet.

2. *A:* How _____ is Dallas from here?

    B: 500 miles.

3. *A:* How _____ is your house?

    B: It has 3 bedrooms and 2 bathrooms.

4. *A:* How _____ do you play tennis?

    B: Once a week.

5. *A:* How _____ is your son?

    B: He's fifteen.

6. *A:* How _____ is that book?

    B: 223 pages.

7. *A:* How _____ do you weigh?★

    B: 145 pounds.

8. *A:* How _____ is Canada?

    B: It's the second biggest country.

★This question can only be asked by a good friend. Otherwise, it is considered very rude.

Part 2.   In each sentence, look at the underlined part carefully. If it is correct, circle the word *correct*. If it is wrong, circle the wrong part and write the correct form above it.

correct   wrong   1. *A:* <u>How long</u> was the meeting?

                            B: It lasted 2 hours.

correct   wrong   2. *A:* <u>How far</u> is Mount Everest?

                            B: I'm not sure, but I think it is the highest mountain in the world.

correct   wrong   3. *A:* <u>How many</u> does it cost?

                            B: $120.

correct   wrong   4. *A:* <u>How difficult</u> was the test?

                            B: It was really difficult. The best score was only 73.

correct   wrong   5. *A:* <u>How usually</u> do you go to the bank?

                            B: I only go two or three times a month.

correct   wrong   6. *A:* <u>What old</u> is Mr. Williamson?

                            B: I think he's about 42.

Unit 6

Adverbs of Frequency

1. *always*
2. *usually*
3. *often*
4. *sometimes*
5. *rarely*
6. *seldom*
7. *never*
8. placement with *be*
9. placement with verbs
10. avoiding double negatives
11. *ever* and *how often* in questions

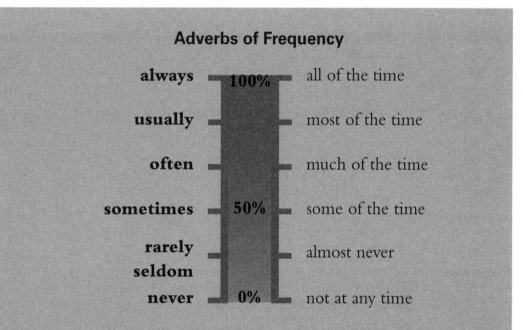

Adverbs of Frequency

always	**100%**	all of the time
usually		most of the time
often		much of the time
sometimes	**50%**	some of the time
rarely		almost never
seldom		
never	**0%**	not at any time

With Verbs

I <u>use</u> a pencil in math class **all of the time.**
He <u>goes</u> to school by bike **most of the time.**
My teacher <u>arrives</u> early **much of the time.**
We <u>play</u> tennis at night **some of the time.**
They **almost never** <u>fail</u> a test.
I don't <u>eat</u> a big breakfast **at any time.**

I **always** <u>use</u> a pencil in math class.
He **usually** <u>goes</u> to school by bike.
My teacher **often** <u>arrives</u> early.
We **sometimes** <u>play</u> tennis at night.
They **rarely** <u>fail</u> a test.
I **never** <u>eat</u> a big breakfast.

With **Be**

In the morning, I <u>am</u> hungry **all of the time.**
He <u>is</u> late to class **most of the time.**
They <u>are</u> **almost never** on time.
We <u>are</u> **not** at school after 5 P.M. **at any time.**

In the morning, I <u>am</u> **always** hungry.
He <u>is</u> **usually** late to class.
They <u>are</u> **seldom** on time.
We <u>are</u> **never** at school after 5 P.M.

Adverbs of frequency: **always, usually, often, sometimes, rarely, seldom, never**

Position: 1. after **be** (I am always tired. She is never late.)
2. before **VERB** (I always arrive on time.)
3. **sometimes** can occur in three positions:
   first: **Sometimes** we play tennis at night.
   middle: We **sometimes** play tennis at night.
   final: We play tennis at night **sometimes**.

CAREFUL! Watch out for these common mistakes.

1. Do not put adverbs of frequency after verbs.
   wrong: Susan calls always her mother.
   correct: Susan always calls her mother.

2. Do not put adverbs of frequency before **be**.
   wrong: I usually am the first person in class.
   correct: I am usually the first person in class.

3. Don't use a negative verb form with **rarely, seldom,** or **never.** These words are
   already negative. Two negatives together is not a possible structure in English.
   wrong: I don't never use a pen in math class.
   correct: I never use a pen in math class.

   wrong: Leo isn't rarely home before 5 P.M.
   correct: Leo is rarely home before 5 P.M.

Exercise 1. Fill in each blank with the correct adverb of frequency and then answer the questions about adverbs of frequency. Follow the example.

1. ___always___ = all of the time   ___100___ % of the time

2. _____ = most of the time

3. _____ = much of the time

4. _____ = some of the time   about _____ % of the time

5. _____ = almost never

6. _____ = almost never

7. _____ = not at any time   _____ % of the time

8. John usually does his homework. Paul always does his homework. Joe never does his

   homework. Who is the best student? _____

9. The weather in Florida is rarely cold. It is sometimes cold in Mississippi. It is usually cold in Alaska. If I don't like cold weather, which state is a good place for me to live?

   _____

10. Nedra seldom walks to work. Carol often walks to work. Betty walks to work sometimes. Who does not walk to work frequently? _____

Exercise 2.   Write a new sentence using a frequency word in place of the bold words. Circle the verbs. Follow the example.

example: He writes letters **all of the time.**
   _He always (writes) letters_____.

1. I study grammar at night **some of the time.**

   _____

2. He studies vocabulary **most of the time.**

   _____

3. We practice pronunciation **all of the time.**

   _____

4. They **almost never** write letters to their parents.

   _____

5. You have coffee for breakfast **all of the time.**

   _____

6. Jack comes to class late **much of the time.**

   _____

7. Mary does **not** sing **at any time.**

   _____

8. We **almost never** speak Spanish in class.

   _____

9. They study at night **much of the time.**

   _____

10. I **don't** eat peanut butter **at any time.** I hate it!

   _____

Bonus Question: Where are the frequency words in relation to the verbs? _____

_____

Exercise 3.   Write a new sentence using a frequency word in place of the bold words. Circle the verbs. Follow the example.

    example: Mary is tired **some of the time.**
           _Mary (is) sometimes tired_____.

1. My first class is at 8 A.M. **all of the time.**

   _____

2. He is hungry **most of the time.**

   _____

3. His letters are **almost never** long.

   _____

4. Bill is **not** absent from Mr. Green's class **at any time.**

   _____

5. Mr. Vince is home **most of the time** when the mail carrier comes.

   _____

6. They're **almost never** in class on Fridays.

   _____

7. I'm nervous before a big tennis match **all of the time.**

   _____

8. Mary's happy **much of the time.**

   _____

9. The teacher is busy in the afternoon **some of the time.**

   _____

10. She is **not** sick **at any time.**

   _____

Bonus Question: Where are the frequency words in relation to the verb *be?* _____

_____

CHALLENGE   A student says the answer for 10 is *She isn't never sick.* Is this correct? Why or why not? You are the teacher now. Can you explain the answer?

Exercise 4.   Underline the correct form. Follow the example.

      example: Marvin (<u>usually comes</u>, comes usually) to class with Sam.

1. Yvonne (never is, is never) sad. She (always seems, seems always) so happy.

2. They (always eat, eat always) at the kitchen table.

3. We (never study, study never) in the morning.

4. He (sometimes is, is sometimes) late for class because he wakes up late.

5. Maria (seldom drinks, drinks seldom) coffee.

6. You (always arrive, arrive always) late for lunch.

7. My teacher (always is, is always) correct.

8. We (seldom speak, speak seldom) Spanish in class because we want to improve our English.

9. You and I (never go, go never) to the bookstore before class.

10. They (seldom are, are seldom) hungry at night.

11. His answers in English class (usually are, are usually) wrong. He isn't good at English.

12. The teacher (always has, has always) his book with him.

13. Breakfast (always is, is always) at 8 A.M.

14. Don (often is, is often) absent from class. He gets sick very easily.

15. She (never studies, studies never), so her grades are not very good.

Grammar: *Ever* and *How Often* in Questions

You can use **ever** in a question. It means "at any time."
You can begin a question with **how often**. It means "how many times."

Joe: "Do you play tennis?"
Tim: "Yes, I do. I like it very much."

Joe: "Do you **ever** play at night?"
Tim: "Yes, but not so much. I prefer to play in the day."

Joe: "**How often** do you play at night?"
Tim: "Maybe once or twice a month."

(See p. 57 for more information on **how often**.)

Exercise 5.   Answer these questions about the information in the chart. Follow the examples.

Name	Play Tennis?	Watch TV?	Eat Vegetables?
Frank	yes/once a week	no/never	yes/two times a day
Audrey	yes/every day	yes/every night	yes/sometimes
Mandy	yes/every day	yes/almost every day	yes/all of the time
Bill	yes/rarely	yes/on Sundays	yes/one meal a day
Debbie	no/never	yes/only at night	no/never

1. Does Audrey ever watch TV?   _Yes, she does._
2. How often does she watch TV?   _Every night._
3. Does Debbie ever eat vegetables?   _____
4. Does Bill ever play tennis?   _____
5. How often does he play tennis?   _____
6. Does Debbie ever watch TV?   _____
7. How often does she watch TV?   _____

Speaking Activity

Exercise 6.   Speaking Activity: Information Questions

Step 1. Write eight questions about the chart in exercise 5. Write the correct answers.

Step 2. Work with a partner. Take turns asking and answering your questions.

1. _____?
   _____.

2. _____?
   _____.

3. _____?
   _____.

4. _____?
   _____.

5. _____ ?

     _____ .

6. _____ ?

     _____ .

7. _____ ?

     _____ .

8. _____ ?

     _____ .

Speaking Activity

Exercise 7.   Speaking Activity. How do you learn new vocabulary? Write the answer that is true for you. (Write *always, usually, often, sometimes, seldom, never.*) Then work with a partner. Take turns asking and answering these questions. Begin each question with "Do you ever . . . ?" If the answer is YES, then ask "How often do you . . . ?"

1. I draw a picture of the meaning.   _____

2. I write the meaning down in a special notebook.   _____

3. I circle new words in different color ink.   _____

4. When I study vocabulary, I repeat the word aloud.   _____

5. I make an example sentence with the new word.   _____

6. I try to use new words in conversation.   _____

7. I look up the meaning of new words in a bilingual dictionary. _____

8. I circle or underline new words when I find them.   _____

9. I write each word several times (perhaps five times).   _____

10. I write a translation of the word next to the English word.   _____

Exercise 8.   Multiple Choice. Circle the letter of the correct answer.

1. "How often do you eat cereal for breakfast?"

    "_____."

    (A) Ever   (C) At all of the time

    (B) Never   (D) Yes, I do

2. He almost never comes to class on time. He _____ always late.

    (A) is   (C) comes

    (B) are   (D) come

3. "Does he ever eat salad for lunch?"

    "Yes, _____."

    (A) always   (C) seldom

    (B) ever   (D) at any time

4. Mr. Hobbs almost never has coffee in the morning. He _____ coffee then.

    (A) seldom has   (C) doesn't seldom have

    (B) has seldom   (D) seldom doesn't have

5. On Monday, he does not come to class. He _____ to class then because he is

    tired.

    (A) ever comes   (C) never comes

    (B) comes ever   (D) comes never

6. "_____ study by yourself?"

    "Yes, I don't like to study with anyone else."

    (A) Ever do you   (C) Do ever you

    (B) Always do you   (D) Do you always

7. "_____ do you read the newspaper?"

    "Almost every day. I like to read it in the morning before I go to work."

    (A) Always   (C) Almost always

    (B) Often how   (D) How often

8. Which sentence is not correct?

    (A) Zina often plays tennis.   (C) The winter is usually very cold here.

    (B) Farah and I often are late.   (D) Meat never costs less than vegetables.

Exercise 9. Review Test

Part 1. Each sentence has two blanks. Fill in one of the blanks in each sentence with the correct adverb of frequency: *always, usually, often, sometimes, rarely, never, ever.* Do not write anything in the other blank in the sentence.

1. I am on time every day. I _____ arrive _____ on time.

2. When you visited Paris, did you _____ go _____ to the Louvre?

3. The teacher wears a tie some of the time. He _____ wears _____ a tie.

4. People _____ eat _____ sugar on scrambled eggs.

5. Tom never fails a test. His score _____ is _____ above 70.

6. Salmon is expensive, so I _____ eat _____ it. The last time was in 1993.

7. Wendy is a very smart student. She _____ makes _____ a mistake on a test.

8. I can't drive, so I _____ drive _____ a car from home to work.

Part 2. Read each sentence carefully. Look at the underlined part. If the underlined part is correct, circle the word *correct*. If it is wrong, circle the wrong part and write the correct form above.

correct wrong   1. She <u>isn't never</u> home between 10 and 11.

correct wrong   2. <u>Do you ever eat</u> breakfast at your friend's house?

correct wrong   3. It <u>usually rains</u> a lot in this area in August.

correct wrong   4. Why <u>do always you sit</u> in the front row in class?

correct wrong   5. Bill <u>is often</u> late for work on Monday.

correct wrong   6. I <u>always read</u> the paper before I go to the office.

correct wrong   7. People drink coffee without sugar or milk <u>rarely</u>.

correct wrong   8. <u>Sometimes</u> we go by bus.

correct wrong   9. Does the teacher <u>ever</u> give short tests?

correct wrong 10. *Bill:* Do you drive to work?
                      Ann: I <u>do always</u>.

Unit 7

Object Pronouns

1. *me*   4. *her*   7. *them*
2. *you*   5. *it*   8. contrast with subject pronouns
3. *him*   6. *us*   9. contrast with possessive adjectives

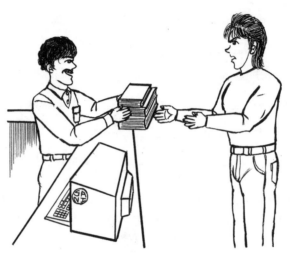

He gave <u>them</u> to <u>him</u>.

Object Pronouns

Subject Pronouns		*Object Pronouns*	
I		me	
you		you	
he		him	
she		her	
it		it	
we		us	
they		them	

I	I play tennis.	**me**	He called me.
	I have a car.		Give the book to me.
you	You sing well.	**you**	I know you.
	You are here.		They live near you.
he	He is French.	**him**	We know him.
	He likes tea.		I study with him.
she	She has a car.	**her**	I telephoned her.
	She runs a lot.		We study with her.

it	It is a radio.		**it**	Do you have it?
	It doesn't eat much.			I write with it.
we	We live here.		**us**	She called us.
	We are students.			She lives near us.
they	They play tennis.		**them**	I know them.
	They are Spanish.			You play tennis with them.

Subject Pronouns: **I, you, he, she, it, we, they**
We use these before a verb. I like tennis. OR They have a car.

Object Pronouns: **me, you, him, her, it, us, them** (*Hint:* **him** and **them** end in **m**)
We use these:
1. after a verb. I called him. OR She helped me.
2. after a preposition.   with me, for him, to you, on them, at her

(Common prepositions: **at, between, by, for, from, in, near, on, to, under, with, without.**)

CAREFUL! Watch out for these common mistakes.

1. Do not use subject pronouns after verbs. Use object pronouns.

   wrong: Andrea called he last night.
   correct: Andrea called him last night.

   wrong: The teacher asked I a question.
   correct: The teacher asked me a question.

2. Do not use subject pronouns after prepositions. Use object pronouns.

   wrong: I ride the bus to school with she every day.
   correct: I ride the bus to school with her every day.

   wrong: Michael and Paul live near we.
   correct: Michael and Paul live near us.

Exercise 1.   Underline the correct words. Follow the example.

1. Please call (I, <u>me</u>) tonight.

2. This book is for (she, her).

3. He sees (I, me), and I see (he, him).

4. Please tell (I, me) your phone number.

5. Do you know (she, her)?

6. Mark lives very near (I, me).

7. I live near the Smiths. I live near (they, them).

8. Bob likes cats. He likes (they, them) a lot.

9. Bob has a cat. He likes (its, it) very much.

10. This book is for (we, us). It is our book.

Exercise 2.   Complete the sentences with the correct object pronoun. Follow the example.

example: I see Susan and Tina. Susan and Tina see __me__ .

1.   Please call John tonight. Please call _____ before 9:30.

2.   We went to the store with Mr. Jones. We went to the store with _____ .

3.   You and I study together. You are a good student. I

     like to study with _____ .

4.   One sandwich is on the table. I am going to eat

     _____ .

5.   Two sandwiches are on the table. I am going to eat

     _____ .

6.   I like fried chicken. Do you like _____ , too?

7.   Fran lives near the school. She lives near _____ .

8.   Vick studied with Keith and me last night. Vick studied with _____ .

9.   I am going to the airport now. I have my suitcase with _____ .

10. Alan is sitting next to Mary. Alan is sitting next to _____ .

Exercise 3.   Complete the sentences with the correct object pronoun. Follow the example.

example: John has a new car. I like __it__ very much.

1.   I know John and Peter very well. I know _____ very well.

2.   Greg lives near Mary. Greg lives near _____ .

3.   John explained the question. He explained _____ .

4.   Mary is eating two sandwiches for lunch. She is eating _____ for lunch.

5.   Michael is leaving now. Does he have his luggage with _____ ?

6.   Can you help _____ ? I need your help.

7.   Do you like these books? I bought _____ at the store near the bank.

8.   Mr. Paulson speaks very fast. Can you understand _____ ?

9.   My boss is Mrs. Williams. Do you know _____ ?

10. This book is for Paul. Please give _____ to _____ tomorrow.

Exercise 4. Write the pronoun and adjective forms. Follow the examples.

Subject Pronoun	Object Pronoun	Possessive Adjective
1. I	8. _me_	15. _my_
2. _____	9. _____	16. your
3. _____	10. him	17. _____
4. she	11. _____	18. _____
5. it	12. _____	19. _____
6. _____	13. _____	20. our
7. they	14. _____	21. _____

Exercise 5. Underline the correct form of the pronoun or adjective. Follow the example.

1. (Me, My, I) have a new car.
2. This sweater is for (he, him, his).
3. (They, Them, Their) last name is Hobbs.
4. (Them, They, Their) are from Ohio.
5. (She, Her) and (she, her) sister are here.
6. (Our, We) begin (us, our) class at 10 A.M.
7. (Our, We, Us) have a test tomorrow.
8. (He, Him) likes cats. (He, Him) has 5 cats.
9. Bob has a cat. (Its, It) is a female cat.
10. Do (you, your) play tennis every day?

Exercise 6. Write the correct form of the pronoun or adjective. Follow the examples.

1. Ann is going to call Bob. __She__ is going to call __him__.
2. John studies with Paul and Joe. _____ studies with _____.
3. Mark studies with Sue. _____ studies with _____.
4. Mary is eating two sandwiches for lunch. _____ is eating _____ for lunch.
5. Mr. and Mrs. Smith live near the school. _____ live near _____.
6. John and I see Mary and you every day. _____ see _____ every day.
7. The girls are going to buy some books. Do _____ have _____ money with _____?

8. We are going to class now. Do _____ have _____ books with

    _____ ?

9. John is leaving. Does _____ have _____ luggage with

    _____ ?

10. Matt and I watched a movie. _____ liked _____ a lot.

Exercise 7.   Finding Errors. Read this short passage. There are seven mistakes.
                   Circle the mistakes and write the correct form above the mistake.

Last night my wife and me had dinner at a restaurant not far from us home. We both

enjoy going there very much because it is a small, friendly place. We go there often, and

the people there know our. Last night the service was not very good. We had to wait a

long time before a waiter came to our table. He was very nice, but he didn't do a very

good job. I ordered chicken with mushrooms, but him brought me chicken with cream

sauce. My wife got its main course OK, but he put the wrong kind of salad dressing on

her salad. We were not happy with the waiter, but we didn't say anything to them. We just

ate what him brought us. Because of these things, we didn't leave a big tip.

Exercise 8.   Object pronouns, Subject Pronouns, Possessive Adjectives. Write C
                   on the line by the correct sentences and X by the wrong sentences.
                   If there is a mistake, circle it and make it correct. (*Hint:* There are
                   twelve sentences. Five are correct, and seven have mistakes.)

_____ 1. I am leaving now. I have me luggage with my.

_____ 2. John and Sue live near the bank. They live near it.

_____ 3. Question number 7 is very difficult. They are very difficult.

_____ 4. Please call John and Sue tonight. Please call they tonight.

_____ 5. Ann is going to call Sammy tonight. He is going to call her

            tonight.

_____ 6. We are going to class now. We have our books with us.

_____ 7. I like to study with he. He is a good student.

_____ 8. Tommy and Kevin are good friends. Them play tennis together every day.

_____ 9. This book is for Paul. Please give it to him tomorrow.

_____ 10. Do you have us telephone number? Please call us tonight.

_____ 11. The Mounties are the Royal Canadian Mounted Police. People can recognize them because of their red coats.

_____ 12. Where is your classroom? Is it on the third floor?

Speaking Activity

Exercise 9.   **Speaking Activity: Pronoun Game**

Step 1. Do either A or B. Do not do both. (A does the left column; B does the right column.)

Step 2. Write the numbers 1–10 on the lines to the left of each column. Mix up the numbers.

Step 3. Now write the correct object pronoun next to each noun. Write *it* or *them* on the line.

Step 4. If you are A, check your answer with another A student. If you are B, work with another B student to check your answers.

Student A		**Student B**	
Number	*Pronoun*	*Number*	*Pronoun*
___ cats	_____	___ pets	_____
___ ice cream	_____	___ cherries	_____
___ winter	_____	___ hot weather	_____
___ flying on a plane	_____	___ cheeseburgers	_____
___ your friends	_____	___ cookies	_____
___ coffee with sugar	_____	___ black coffee	_____
___ sports cars	_____	___ green	_____
___ red shoes	_____	___ cigarettes	_____
___ math	_____	___ homework	_____
___ tests	_____	___ going on a picnic	_____

Step 5. The teacher will say "Go" and then say "Stop" one minute later. Student A will begin to read his or her list of nouns one at a time following the numbers on the left side of the column. Student B must listen to the noun and then say "I really don't like *it* very much" or "I really don't like *them* very much." (Student B should close the book while student A is talking.)

Step 6. If the object pronoun is correct, then A will say, "Oh, really, I didn't know that." If the object pronoun is not correct, then A will say, "No, that's not correct" and go to the next noun.

Step 7. The object of this game is to say as many miniconversations as possible in the time limit.

Step 8. Change roles. The teacher will time the activity again as student B reads his or her list and student A responds.

Exercise 10.   Multiple Choice. Circle the letter of the correct answer.

1. "Is this your coat?"

    "Yes, my mother gave it to _____ last year."

    (A) my   (C) I

    (B) me   (D) I am

2. His last name doesn't have 12 letters. _____ only has 11.

    (A) He   (C) It

    (B) Him   (D) Its

3. "I work at Brooklyn Bank on Green Street."

    "Oh, then you probably know John and Susan. _____ work at that same bank."

    (A) They   (C) Them

    (B) Their   (D) They're

4. "Where did _____ keys?"

    "I put your keys on the table. Aren't they there now?"

    (A) I put your   (C) you put my

    (B) your put my   (D) me me your

5. "Excuse me, I'd like to speak to Mr. Nakano."

    "I'm sorry, but he's not here right now. Do you want to leave a message for _____?"

    (A) his   (C) he

    (B) he's   (D) him

6. "Hi, Mark and Lee. Why are you guys late?"

    "Well, _____ bus was a little late today."

    (A) us   (C) we

    (B) our   (D) my

7. Pamela forgot to take _____ when she left the house this morning.

    (A) her wallet with she   (C) her wallet with her

    (B) she wallet with she   (D) she's wallet with her

8. "What did Ahmad say about the movie?"

    "He said _____ liked it very much."

    (A) his   (C) him

    (B) he's   (D) he

Exercise 11.   Review Test

Part 1.   Read these sentences. Fill in the blanks with any word that makes sense but try to use a pronoun.

1. There was a poor man standing in front of the store. John gave the man a sandwich.

   He gave _____ to _____ because the man didn't have anything to eat.

2. The teacher was angry at all the students in my class. She was angry at _____

   because we were talking so much.

3. Math is my favorite class. I like _____ because I'm good at numbers.

4. Susan likes English and science. These classes are easy for _____.

5. Sometimes I call up Frank, and sometimes Frank calls _____.

Part 2.   Read each sentence carefully. Look at the underlined part. If the underlined part is correct, circle the word *correct*. If it is wrong, circle the wrong part and write the correct form above.

correct	wrong	1. This book looks interesting, so I might buy <u>them</u>.
correct	wrong	2. Jill took her umbrella with <u>her</u> because it was raining really hard.
correct	wrong	3. It's impossible for <u>she</u> to arrive here early in the morning.
correct	wrong	4. John is my best friend. I met <u>her</u> in 1992.
correct	wrong	5. Mr. and Mrs. Smith needed my help, so I helped <u>them</u>.
correct	wrong	6. My name is easy to say, but people can't spell <u>it</u>.
correct	wrong	7. The T-shirts in that store are nice, but some of <u>them</u> are expensive.
correct	wrong	8. Mr. Fernandez taught Lee and <u>I</u> to play tennis.
correct	wrong	9. The teacher told <u>we</u> that our tests were not good.
correct	wrong	10. Paul gave the watch to <u>me</u> for my birthday.

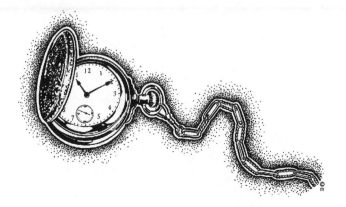

Unit 8

One and *Other*

1. *one* vs. *it*   2. *other:* *another, other, others*   3. *other:* *the other, the others*

> Do you want this book?

> No, give me <u>the other</u> book, please.

---

it and *one*

it

Bob: "What is the name of the store?"
Ann: "It's Rainbow Connection."

Ben: "Do you like your grammar class?"
Sue: "No, I don't like it."

Use ***it*** for something specific.

one

Mike: "Do you have a car?"
Pam: "Yes, I have one."

Tom: "I need an eraser."
Wes: "Sure. There's one in the top drawer."

Use ***one*** for something general.

Exercise 1.   Write *it* or *one* on the lines. Follow the example.

example: Tom: "Do you have a car?"
            Ben: "No, I don't have ___one___."

1. Tom: "Do you know the answer to question number 12?"

   Ben: "No, I don't know _____. Do you know _____?"

2. *Vick:* "Did you do the homework?"

   Anna: "No, I didn't do _____."

3. *Jay:* "I need a knife to cut these potatoes."

   Jim: "You can find _____ in that drawer."

4. *Pam:* "Do you want to eat a cheeseburger?"

   Carl: "No, thanks. I ate _____ for lunch today. I don't think I can eat the

   same thing twice in one day."

5. *Anna:* "Is that a new chair?"

   Sam: "No, _____'s old. I bought _____ several years ago."

6. *Tim:* "Do you need a pen?"

   Rick: "Yes, I do. Please give me _____."

7. *Henry:* "I can't find my book."

   Jimmy: "There's _____ here on the floor. Is this your book?"

   Henry: "Yes, that's _____."

8. *Dan:* "What kind of car is that?"

   Mary: "_____ is a Toyota."

Other

	Singular	*Plural*
General	another _____ (another one) (another)	other _____s (other ones) (others)
	Joe: "I drank two glasses of water, but I'm still thirsty." *Bob:* "Do you want another glass?"	*Joe:* "Are you the only student in your class who is seventeen?" *Sue:* "No, there are others."
	Another has the idea of one more. It is singular.	**Other** + PLURAL NOUN (or just **others**) is similar, but the idea is plural.
Specific	the other _____ (the other one) (the other)	the other _____s (the other ones) (the others)

Joe: "Tell me about your teachers." *Bob:* "I have two teachers. One is from New York, and the other one is from Florida."	*Joe:* "Tell me about your teachers." *Bob:* "I have five teachers. One is from New York, and the other ones are from Florida."
The other has the idea of the last one in a group. It is singular. It is specific.	**The other + PLURAL NOUN** (or just **the others**) is similar, but the idea is plural. It is specific.

CAREFUL! Watch out for these common mistakes.

1. Do not use **other** for singular nouns. Use **another** or **the other.**

   wrong: I have other dictionary at home.
   correct: I have another dictionary at home.

   wrong: G-r-e-y is one way to spell this word. What is other way?
   correct: G-r-e-y is one way to spell this word. What is the other way?

2. Do not use **other** by itself.

   wrong: Please give me other.
   correct: Please give me another.
   correct: Please give me the other.

3. Do not use two plural words.

   wrong: There are others books on the bottom shelf.
   correct: There are other books on the bottom shelf.

   wrong: Two children are absent today, but the others children are here.
   correct: Two children are absent today, but the other children are here.

Exercise 2.   Underline the correct words. Follow the example.

   example: I have two nice shirts. This one is white, and (other, another,
   <u>the other</u>) one is green.

1. I'm thirsty. Can I have (another, other) soft drink?

2. Some people arrived at noon. (Another, Other, Others) came at one.

3. The morning manager at the restaurant is Chris. The night manager is Bob. Chris is

   very nice, but (another, the other, other) manager is very strict.

4. If you want to talk to me (another, other) time about this situation, just let me know.

5. The first and last letters in "read" are consonants, but (another, the other, others, the

   others) are vowels.

6. This is the only difficult test. All the (others, another, other) tests are easy.

7. This is the only difficult test. All the (others, another, other) ones are easy.

8. This is the only difficult test. All the (others, another, other) are easy.

9. Cats and monkeys are mammals. Bears and kangaroos are (others, another, other) examples.

10. The first three letters of the word are t, h, and i, but I can't read (other, another, the other, others) one.

Exercise 3.   Write *another one* or *the other one* on the line. Follow the example.

         example: I have a pen here on the table. I have __another one__ in my car.

1. Mary is writing a letter now. She is going to write _____ tomorrow.

2. Mary needs to write two letters. She's going to write one now. Then she's going to write _____ tomorrow.

3. I'm going to buy two shirts. I'm going to buy one today, and I'm going to buy _____ tomorrow.

4. John's reading a book now. He wants to read _____ next week.

5. I have three cats. Two of them are black, and _____ is white.

6. I have many books. I really like books a lot. I'm going to buy _____ next Saturday when I go to the mall.

7. Mary has four books. Two are grammar books, and one is a reading book. _____ is a writing book.

8. I am reading a book now. Tomorrow I'm going to read _____.

9. She has two sisters. One is short, and _____ is tall.

10. I have two pens in my left hand. There is _____ on the table. So there are three pens altogether. Two of them have blue ink, but _____ has black ink.

Exercise 4.   Write *another one, the other one, other, others,* or *the others* on the
lines. Follow the example.

        example: I bought a shirt today. I'm going to buy <u> another one </u>
                 tomorrow.

1. I have a pen here on the table. I have _____ in my car. The

    pen on the table is old, and _____ is new.

2. Mary bought three apples. She ate two of the apples. Now she is going to eat

    _____.

3. We have two pages of homework. I did one page last night, and I'm going to do

    _____ in a few minutes.

4. Many students speak English. A few _____ speak French.

5. Five people came to class. One has his book, but _____ don't

    have their books.

6. Susan has two classes. She's attending one now. She's going to go to

    _____ after lunch.

7. A few students arrive late every day. A few _____ arrive on

    time.

8. Many students don't eat breakfast. Many _____ students don't

    eat lunch.

9. I have two pens. I don't like this pen. I prefer _____.

10. Jimmy has two brothers. One is in Nigeria, and _____ is in

    Egypt.

11. Four men work here at night. Four _____ work here in the

    day.

12. The park has many children in it now. One child is flying a kite.

    _____ is sailing a toy boat. Some _____

    are playing football.

Exercise 5. Write *another one, the other one, other, others,* or *the others* on the lines. Follow the example.

example: I called one of my friends yesterday. I'm calling __another one__ now.

1. A few students study in the morning. Many _____ students study at night.

2. One student is standing near the door. _____ is sitting at his desk.

3. *A:* Listen! Susan's singing a song.

   B: Her voice isn't very good. I hope she doesn't sing any _____.

4. Kevin has two pens. He doesn't like this pen so much. He likes _____ more.

5. Karen has two sisters. One is in Canada, and _____ is in Mexico.

6. Fifteen men work here at night. Ten _____ work here in the day.

7. The library has many students in it now. One student is writing a letter. _____ is studying math. Some _____ are talking.

8. I'm going to write three letters. I'm writing two letters now, and I'm going to write _____ tomorrow.

9. I have a lot of good books. They are excellent. This one is about history. It's the only one about history. All the _____ books are about science.

10. I'm going to buy two T-shirts. I'm going to buy one today, and I'm going to buy _____ tomorrow.

11. Gregory's reading a history book now. He really loves history, so it's no surprise that he wants to read _____ next week.

12. I have three kittens. Two of them are light brown, and _____ is dark gray.

CHALLENGE A student says the answer for 12 is *the other one,* but another student says the answer is *another one.* One answer is wrong. You are the teacher now. Can you explain which answer is correct and why?

Speaking Activity

Exercise 6.   Speaking Activity

Step 1. Work with a partner. One of you is responsible for A, and the other is responsible for B.

Step 2. Read the pair of sentences. There are an A sentence and a B sentence. Both have an underlined part. Which one is correct and which one is wrong?

Step 3. Circle the letter of the wrong sentence. Then write your reason on the line.

Step 4. Compare your answers. Discuss any differences. Can you both explain why you say a sentence is wrong? *Remember:* One student is responsible for explaining the A sentences, and the other student is responsible for explaining the B sentences.

1. (A)   Those sandwiches look delicious. I would like to eat <u>the other one</u>.

   (B)   I enjoyed my trip to Miami last month. I want to go there <u>another time</u>.

   Reason: _____

2. (A)   Some people like fish, but <u>others</u> hate it.

   (B)   There is a book on the desk, and there is <u>other</u> on the sofa.

   Reason: _____

3. (A)   The teacher was sick, so <u>another</u> teacher came to our class today.

   (B)   Please give me <u>other</u> glass of water. I'm so thirsty!

   Reason: _____

4. (A)   The test had 10 questions. Number 1 was easy, but <u>the another ones</u> were hard.

   (B)   She has 2 brothers. One lives in Miami, and <u>the other</u> is in Philadelphia.

   Reason: _____

5. (A)   For our next vacation, let's go to Paris. <u>Another</u> good place might be London.

   (B)   <u>Another</u> telephone numbers for the bank are 234-9921 and 234-9922.

   Reason: _____

6. (A)   A student can only use this computer for 1 hour if there are <u>other</u> students waiting.

   (B)   The plate was not clean, so I asked the waitress to bring me <u>other</u> plate.

   Reason: _____

Exercise 7.   Multiple Choice. Circle the letter of the correct answer.

1. *Joe:*   "Did you buy a pencil yesterday?"

   Don: "No, but I'm going to buy _____ today."

   (A) it   (C) some

   (B) one   (D) other

2. Four men work here in the morning, and four _____ work here in the evening.

   (A) ones   (C) others ones

   (B) others   (D) the others

3. *Tim:*   "One of the students is reading a book."

   Meg: "What are _____ doing?"

   Tim: "They're reading, too."

   (A) the other one   (C) the others

   (B) the others ones   (D) another one

4. I have five cats. Four are black, and _____ is gray.

   (A) four   (C) the other

   (B) it   (D) another

5. *Jill:*   "May I use this green pen?"

   Penny: "No, please don't use _____."

   (A) it   (C) one

   (B) another   (D) the other

6. I have a yellow pencil here on the table, and I have a few _____ in my car.

   (A) another   (C) others

   (B) anothers   (D) others ones

7. *Tina:*   "Would you like an apple?"

   Rita: "Yes, I'd like _____."

   (A) one   (C) it

   (B) an   (D) another

8. There _____ on the table.

   (A) is other book   (C) is another books

   (B) are other books   (D) are the other book

Exercise 8.   Review Test

Part 1.   Read these sentences. Fill in the blanks with these words: *one, it, other, another, others, the other, the others.*

1. John gave the man a sandwich. He gave _____ to him because the man didn't have anything to eat.

2. One possible reason for your bad grade is that the test was too difficult, but there are many _____ possible reasons.

3. A rainbow has six colors in it. _____ of these colors is red. Blue and yellow are two _____.

4. There are two sandwiches on the table. This one has cheese, but _____ doesn't have cheese.

5. They played a hockey game yesterday. They had a good time, so they want to play _____ one tomorrow or the next day.

6. Florida has four large cities. Three of them are Miami, Orlando, and Jacksonville. _____ large city in Florida is Tampa.

7. Ahmad has three cats. The oldest cat is white, but _____ are gray and white.

8. I did my homework, but I left _____ on my desk. I hope the teacher isn't angry about this.

Part 2.   Read each sentence carefully. Look at the underlined part. If the underlined part is correct, circle the word *correct*. If it is wrong, circle the wrong part and write the correct form above.

correct   wrong   1. This painting looks interesting, so I might buy <u>one</u>.

correct   wrong   2. I have two watches. One is gold, and <u>the other</u> is silver.

correct   wrong   3. A few students arrived late, but many <u>others</u> students came on time.

correct   wrong   4. This pen doesn't write. I need <u>another one</u>.

correct   wrong   5. Brenda has four teachers. Two of them are from Colorado, and <u>the another one is</u> from New York.

correct   wrong   6. Dan and Sue are in their blue car now, but they have <u>another one</u> at home.

correct   wrong   7. Cats and monkeys are mammals. Tigers and lions are <u>others</u> examples.

correct   wrong   8. Have a safe trip home! And please come visit me <u>other</u> time.

Unit 9

Possessive

1. *'s* vs. *of*
2. *'s* vs. *s'*
3. *whose* to ask possession
4. possessive pronouns: *mine, yours,* etc.

Possessive

's *(apostrophe)*	**of**
John has a book.	This book has a title.
It is John**'s** book.	The title **of** this book has five words.
John has books.	This table has legs.
They are John**'s** books.	The legs **of** this table are very strong.
The boys have toys.	I liked the movie. The end was good.
The boy**s'** toys are on the floor.	The end **of** the movie was good.
The boy has toys.	London is in England. It is the capital.
The boy**'s** toys are on the floor.	London is the capital **of** England.

There are two ways to show possession in English: **'s** or **of.**

1. **'s** is used with people: Bob's car, the man's name, the girls' toys

    's is used with some time words: today's newspaper, tomorrow's weather

If the noun is singular, add **'s**:	the boy	the boy**'s** name
If the noun ends in **s,** add **'**:	the boys	the boys' names
If a proper noun★ ends in **s,**	James	James' sweater
you can add **'** or **'s**.		James**'s** sweater

★A proper noun is the name of a person, place, or thing: James, Boston, Pepsi.

2. **of** is used with things: the name of the hotel, the color of this car

3. **'s** or **of** can be used with animals, but we often use **'s**: my cat's name OR the name of my cat

4. **'s** or **of** can be used with words that mean groups of people: city, country; the city's problems OR the problems of the city

Asking a Question about Possession: **whose**

To ask about the owner of something, we use **whose**:

A: Whose books are those?   A: Whose watch is this?

B: They're John's.   B: It's Susan's.

OR: They're John's books.   OR: It's Susan's watch.

Note: It is not necessary to use a noun after **whose** if it is clear in the conversation.

Two people are pointing to a cat: A: Oh, no! There's a cat by the door! I'm afraid of cats!

                                        B: Whose is it? Is it Mr. Miller's cat? Is it a stray cat?

Possessive Pronouns

We can also use a possessive pronoun instead of a possessive adjective + **NOUN.** The possessive pronouns are **mine, yours, his, hers, its, ours, theirs.** Remember that all of these end in *-s* (except **mine**). Also, there is no difference in English between singular or plural with possessive pronouns.

It's my book.	It's mine.	It's our cat.	It's ours.
It's your car.	It's yours.	They're your books.	They're yours.
It's his watch.	It's his.	Those are their cats.	Those are theirs.
It's her house.	It's hers.		

CAREFUL! Watch out for these common mistakes.

1. Use **of** with things. Do not use **'s** or **'**.
   wrong: The book's price is $27.
   correct: The price of the book is $27.

   wrong: This hotel's location is not good.
   correct: The location of this hotel is not good.

2. Use **'s** or **'** with people and some time words (**today, yesterday**). Do not use **of**.
   wrong: The car of Dan is green.
   correct: Dan's car is green.

wrong:	The name of the new girl is Patsy.
correct:	The new girl's name is Patsy.

wrong:	The homework of yesterday was difficult.
correct:	Yesterday's homework was difficult.

3. Don't use **the** with the name of a person + **'s.**
   - wrong: The car is Mary's. It is the Mary's car.
   - correct: The car is Mary's. It is Mary's car.

4. Do not confuse possessive pronouns with possessive adjectives. A pronoun cannot be used in front of a noun.
   - wrong: That is mine tennis racket.
   - correct: That is my tennis racket. (OR: That tennis racket is mine.)

Exercise 1.   Circle the letter of the usual possessive form. Follow the example.

> *example:*   (A) the man's house
> (B) the house of the man

1. (A) the table's top
   (B) the top of the table

2. (A) the monkey's tail
   (B) the tail of the monkey

3. (A) the machine's work
   (B) the work of the machine

4. (A) the table's legs
   (B) the legs of the table

5. (A) Terry's car
   (B) the car of Terry

6. (A) the girls' books
   (B) the books of the girls

7. (A) today's news program
   (B) the news program of today

8. (A) the desk's color
   (B) the color of the desk

9. (A) Frank's dictionary
   (B) the dictionary of Frank

10. (A) the students' test papers
    (B) the test papers of the students

Exercise 2.   Write the correct possessive form. Follow the examples.

Sentence	*Topic*
1. Keith has a car.	Keith's car
2. The box has a cover.	the cover of the box
3. The child has a toy.	_____
4. John has a pencil.	_____

5. The woman has a ring.   _____

6. I bought this newspaper today.   _____

7. The pencil has a point.   _____

8. The car belongs to Tim.   _____

9. The story has a beginning.   _____

10. Mr. Smith has a tie.   _____

11. The homework is for tomorrow.   _____

12. The city has a problem.   _____

13. Ned owns a house.   _____

14. The secretary does work.   _____

15. Andrea has a hobby.   _____

Exercise 3.   Combine the two sentences. Write the correct possessive form. Follow the example.

> *example:*   Carol owns a house. It is large.
> <u>Carol's house is large.</u>

1. Keith has a car. It is green.

   _____

2. The pencil is on the table. Jim owns the pencil.

   _____

3. Jennifer owns a ring. It is gold.

   _____

4. The books belong to Mark. They are on the desk by the door.

   _____

5. The coins are very old. The coins belong to Mr. Nelson.

   _____

6. Dr. Guilford has a nice office. It is at the corner of Green Street and Lincoln Avenue.

   _____

Exercise 4.   Speaking Activity: Possession Drill

Step 1. Do either A or B. Do not do both. (A does the left column; B does the right column.)
Step 2. Write the numbers 1–5 on the lines to the left of each column. Mix up the numbers.
Step 3. Now fill in the long lines with the correct possessive forms.
Step 4. If you are A, check your answer with another A student. If you are B, work with another B student to check your answers.
Step 5. When you finish, then an A student should work with a B student.

Fill in the long lines with the correct possessive form. Follow the examples.

examples: John/a car = ___John's car___
               the table/the legs = ___the legs of the table___

Student A	Student B
____ a new house/George =	____ Jack/a story =
____ Karen/English =	____ the lunch/today =
____ the homework/tonight =	____ this shirt/the price =
____ the color/the house =	____ the name/my cat =
____ England/the queen =	____ the book/the cover =

CHALLENGE   The teacher asked a student to explain how to express possession in English. The student answered, "You can always use *of* for possession. You can say *the top of the table* and you can say *the house of Mr. and Mrs. Miller.* If you want, you can also use *'s* for people. You can say *Mary's book.*" The teacher was not happy with this explanation. Why not?

Exercise 5.   Speaking Activity: Making Original Sentences. Use the same cues
               from exercise 4, but this time your partner must make a sentence
               from the cues you give. Listen to your partner's sentence. Say if it is
               correct or not. Follow the examples.

examples: *You say:*   John/a car
               Your partner says: John's car is green. OR
                                    I like John's car.
               You say: Correct. OR
                                    That's right. OR
                                    No, try again.

               Your partner says: the table/the legs
               You say: The legs of the table are brown. OR
                                    Can you see the legs of the table?
               You say: Correct. OR
                                    That's right. OR
                                    No, try again.

Exercise 6a.   Speaking Activity: Family Tree—Student A. Work with a partner. You
               and your partner will work together to fill in the family tree below.
               Student A should work on this page. Student B should work on
               page 97. Ask student B questions to find out the names of the
               missing people in this family tree.

examples: Who is Theo's wife? OR What is Theo's wife's name?

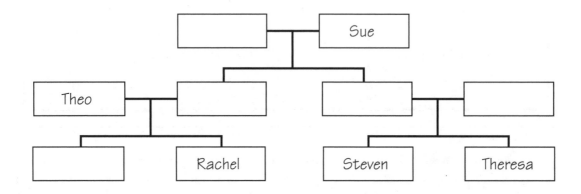

Speaking Activity

Exercise 6b.   Speaking Activity: Family Tree—Student B. Work with a partner. You and your partner will work together to fill in the family tree below. Student B should work on this page. Student A should work on page 96. Ask student A questions to find out the names of the missing people in this family tree.

examples: Who is Carl's wife? OR What is Carl's wife's name?

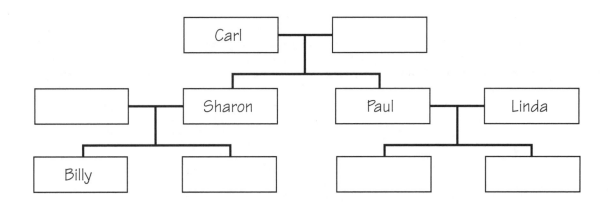

Exercise 7.   Write ten sentences about the people on the tree in exercise 6. Write five true statements and five false statements. Write True or False on the line. Then take turns reading your statements in pairs or small groups. The other students have to say whether your statements are true or false. Follow the examples.

<u>False</u> A. <u>Rachel is Paul's wife.</u>

<u>True</u>   B. <u>Linda's husband's name is Paul.</u>

_____ 1. _____

_____ 2. _____

_____ 3. _____

_____ 4. _____

_____ 5. _____

_____ 6. _____

_____ 7. _____

_____ 8. _____

_____ 9. _____

_____ 10. _____

Exercise 8.   Multiple Choice. Circle the letter of the correct answer.

1. "Did you buy the table?"

   "No, I didn't. _____ were not strong."

   (A) The legs the table   (C) The table's legs

   (B) The legs of the table   (D) The table of the legs

2. These are not my books. These are _____.

   (A) the books of Henry   (C) Henry's books

   (B) Henry's the books   (D) the books of Henry's

3. "What are you reading?"

   "_____."

   (A) The newspaper of today   (C) The newspaper's today

   (B) Today the newspaper's   (D) Today's newspaper

4. "Who is that boy in the green sweater?"

   "_____ is Vic Richards. He's new."

   (A) The boy's name   (C) The name of the boy

   (B) The name's boy   (D) The boy of the name

5. "Let's buy this cake."

   "That's a good idea. Excuse me, what is _____?"

   (A) the price of this cake   (C) the price's cake

   (B) the cake of this price   (D) the cake's price

6. "Of all the students in our class, who speaks English the best?"

   "I think _____ is the best."

   (A) the English of Carrine   (C) Carrine's English

   (B) Carrine's the English   (D) the English's Carrine

7. "Which house is yours?"

   "That one over there. The white house on the corner. That's _____."

   (A) mine house   (C) my house's

   (B) mine   (D) my

8. "_____?"

   "It's Susan's."

   (A) Whose is that car   (C) Who is that car

   (B) Whose car is that   (D) Who that car is

Exercise 9.   Review Test

Part 1.   Read this short passage. Fill in the blanks with any word or words that make sense.

This is Luke Walker. He is standing in front of his house. You can see his car in front of

his house. The man next to Luke is his father. Luke's father's name is Len.

Do you like _____? It is about five years old. _____ is not
                        (Luke/house)   (Luke/house)
very old, so the house is still in good condition.

What do you think about _____? Do you like it?
                                            (Luke/house/color)
Luke painted his house white because it's a good color for a house. Do you agree?

What do you think about _____? The house is not
                                            (size/house)
very big, but it was not very expensive. _____ was very
                                                                    (price/house)
good. He only paid $45,000.

Part 2. Read this short passage. There are five mistakes. Circle the mistakes and write the correct form above the mistake.

This book is very interesting. The name of the book is *The Dead Body.* It is about a murder in a small town. The town's name is Brookley.

I bought this book at the bookstore on Green Street. The book's price was $27. I don't think this book is expensive. The price of the book is all right.

The Dead Body was written by Meg Gibson. This is not the first book of Gibson. She wrote another book that was very famous. That book's name is *The Magic Monster in the Mountain.* The pronunciation of this title is a little difficult for some people.

Gibson's books are very interesting. I hope you will read Gibsons' books some day.

Part 3. Read each sentence carefully. Look at the underlined part. If the underlined part is correct, circle the word *correct.* If it is wrong, circle the wrong part and write the correct form above.

correct   wrong   1. The class of Mary and Jan is not very big.

correct   wrong   2. What's this cake's price?

correct   wrong   3. Is your name on the front of the envelope?

correct   wrong   4. Tomorrow's homework is not very difficult.

correct   wrong   5. Do you know this ice cream's name?

correct   wrong   6. The boys' books are on the table.

correct   wrong   7. When is the last day of John at the office?

Unit 10

Comparative and Superlative

1. *more/the most* vs. *er/the . . . est*
2. important irregular forms
3. avoiding double comparisons
4. use of *than* in comparisons

big   bigger   the biggest

Comparative and Superlative

more . . ./the most . . .

There are three books.
Book A is **expensive.**
Book B is **more expensive** than Book A.
Book C is **the most expensive** (of all).

I think basketball is **interesting**.
I think soccer is **more interesting**.
I think tennis is **the most interesting**.

intelligent	quickly
more intelligent	more quickly
the most intelligent	the most quickly

Use **more** when there are two things/people.

Use **the most** when there are three or more.

er/the . . . est

Mark has a brother, Joe, and a sister, Ann.
Mark is **tall**.
Joe is **taller** than Mark.
Ann is **the tallest** (of all).

Algeria is **big**.
The United States is **bigger** than Algeria.
Canada is **the biggest** of all three.

happy	nice
happier	nicer
the happiest	the nicest

Use **er** when there are two things/people.

Use **the . . . est** when there are three or more.

101

Use **more** and **the most** with:	Use **er** and **the . . . est** with:
1. adjectives that have three or more syllables: expensive	1. adjectives that have one syllable: big
2. adverbs that end in **ly:** quickly	2. adjectives that have two syllables and end in **y:** easy
3. adjectives that have two syllables: famous	

Irregular:	good	→	better	→	the best
	well	→	better	→	the best
	bad	→	worse	→	the worst
	badly	→	worse	→	the worst
	far	→	farther	→	the farthest

CAREFUL! Watch out for these common mistakes.

1. Do not mix up when to use **er** and when to use **more**.

   wrong: I am more busy at work in the morning than in the afternoon.
   correct: I am busier at work in the morning than in the afternoon.

   wrong: I think blue is beautifuller than red for a car.
   correct: I think blue is more beautiful than red for a car.

2. Do not mix up when to use **the . . . est** and **the most**.

   wrong: All the students are smart, but Sam is the most smart.
   correct: All the students are smart, but Sam is the smartest.

   wrong: Of all the tests in this class, yesterday's test was the difficultest.
   correct: Of all the tests in this class, yesterday's test was the most difficult.

3. Be careful with the irregular forms. Don't use the wrong form.

   wrong: The location of that hotel is more bad than this one.
   correct: The location of that hotel is worse than this one.

   wrong: Which is the goodest for the party: carrots, potatoes, or tomatoes?
   correct: Which is the best for the party: carrots, potatoes, or tomatoes?

4. Don't use double comparisons.

   wrong: This color is more darker than that one.
   correct: This color is darker than that one.

   wrong: Jan sings more better than Harriet.
   correct: Jan sings better than Harriet.

5. Don't forget to use **than** with comparative forms.

   wrong: She is taller from her sister.
   correct: She is taller than her sister.

   wrong: Gina's paper was more detailed that Sue's paper.
   correct: Gina's paper was more detailed than Sue's paper.

Exercise 1.   Put a check mark in the parentheses (√) by the correct comparative forms. Follow the examples.

         examples: (√) more careful   ( ) oftener   (√) quicker

1. ( ) taller   5. ( ) more rapidly   9. ( ) badder

2. ( ) more important   6. ( ) better   10. ( ) sooner

3. ( ) more noisy   7. ( ) more nice   11. ( ) more difficult

4. ( ) clearlier   8. ( ) necessarier   12. ( ) more far

Exercise 2.   Write the correct comparative forms. Follow the example.

         example: Gary is rich. Joe is very rich. Joe is <u> richer than </u> Gary.

1. Jill is five feet tall. Martha is six feet tall. Martha is _____ Jill.

2. This book is expensive. That book is cheap. This book is _____ that book.

3. Greg's score was good. Paul's score was very good. Paul's score was _____ Greg's.

4. Ken drives carefully. Matt drives very carefully. Matt drives _____ Ken.

5. Maya is twenty-one years old. Karen is thirty years old. Karen is _____ Maya.

6. Their cat is bad. Our cat is really bad. Our cat is_____ their cat.

7. Mike is intelligent. His sister is extremely intelligent. Mike's sister is _____ he is.

8. The length of this table is four feet. The length of that table is six feet. That table is _____ this table.

9. It's fifty miles to Miami. It's eight hundred miles to Atlanta. Atlanta is _____ Miami.

10. That box is heavy, but this box isn't. That box is _____ this box.

Exercise 3.   Put a check mark in the parentheses (√) by the correct superlative forms. Follow the examples.

      examples: ( ) the most happy   (√) the most careful
                (√) the quickest

1. ( ) the most elegant   5. ( ) the most expensive   9. ( ) the saddest

2. ( ) the goodest   6. ( ) the most busy   10. ( ) the most rapidly

3. ( ) the worst   7. ( ) the easiliest   11. ( ) the most wise

4. ( ) the most quickly   8. ( ) the quickest   12. ( ) the farthest

Exercise 4.   Complete these sentences with the correct superlative forms. Follow the example.

      example: I like ice cream. Vanilla is good, but I like strawberry better. However, I think chocolate is _the best_   kind of ice cream.

1. A plastic watch is not expensive. A silver watch is more expensive. Of course a gold watch is _____ watch.

2. I'm hungry, but I don't have much time to cook. Eating spaghetti is fast, but eating canned beans is faster. However, just eating sandwiches is _____ .

3. Toyotas are very good cars. Even an old Toyota is a little expensive. A new small Toyota is more expensive. But a new Toyota with dual air bags and other modern items is _____ .

4. The dinner at that restaurant was great. The fresh salad was delicious, and the soup was even more delicious than the fresh salad. But my favorite was the dessert. I think that the chocolate cake was _____ food that I ate last night.

5. Some people prefer to pay with cash. Others prefer to pay by check because it's more convenient. However, credit cards are _____ form of payment to me.

6. The are many large parks in the world, but these parks are not usually in urban (city)

    areas. Pacific Spirit Park is around the University of British Columbia in Vancouver.

    It is _____ urban park in the world.

Exercise 5.   Write the correct forms on the lines. Follow the examples.

He is _____.	*I am* _____.	*She is* _____.
1. tall	taller	the tallest
2. careful		
3. good		
4. nice		
5. smart		
6. far		

He paints _____.	*I paint* _____.	*She paints* _____.
7. slowly		
8. rapidly		
9. badly		
10. quickly		

Exercise 6.   Put a check mark (√) on the line by the correct form. Follow the example.

    example: _√_ A. the man's house
                   ___ B. the house of the man

1. ___ A. heavier	6. ___ A. successfuller
___ B. more heavy	___ B. more successful
2. ___ A. more pleasant	7. ___ A. more serious
___ B. pleasanter	___ B. seriouser
3. ___ A. the most quick	8. ___ A. the most colorful
___ B. the quickest	___ B. the colorfullest
4. ___ A. the most quickly	9. ___ A. the most bad
___ B. the quickliest	___ B. the worst
5. ___ A. more interesting	10. ___ A. the slowliest
___ B. interestinger	___ B. the most slowly

Exercise 7.   Write the correct form of the word on the line. Read the situation
               carefully. Some sentences use comparative or superlative forms,
               but some do not. Follow the examples.

examples: (old)   John is _older than_____ Pete, but Mary is
                            _the oldest_____ .
              (quickly)   She drives very _quickly_____ .
              (spicy)   I don't like _spicy_____ food.

1. (tall)   Katie is _____ Paul, but Jill is _____.

2. (good)   She is _____ student in the entire class.

3. (happy)   Mark won first place in the race yesterday. Of course he was

                   _____ person there.

4. (interesting) I do not think this novel is _____. In fact, I think that

                   the author's last novel was much _____ this novel.

5. (difficult)   Which is _____ for you—math or English?

6. (pretty)   Which of these do you think is _____ baby?

7. (nice)   Mr. Woods is very _____, but Mr. Nichols is

                   _____ Mr. Woods.

8. (bad)   My last test was really _____, but I think that today's

                   test was _____. My last score was 55, but today's score

                   was only 43.

9. (easy)   Reading a magazine is _____ reading a science book.

10. (cold)   We can't go swimming today because it's too _____.

                   Today it's much _____ it was yesterday.

11. (tall)   I am not _____. I have two sisters. My sister Brenda is

                   _____ person in our family. She is

                   _____ I am. She is _____ than our

                   parents.

12. (large)   Many people know that Texas and California are _____

                   states. They also know that Texas is _____ California.

                   However, some people believe that Texas is _____ state

                   in the United States. This is not correct. _____ state in

                   the United States is Alaska.

Speaking Activity

Exercise 8.   Speaking Activity: Grammar Drill

Step 1.   The box below has thirty-six adjectives and adverbs. Choose any fifteen of them.

Step 2.   Write them on the top lines by the numbers. Then write the correct comparative and superlative forms under each word. Follow the example in number 1.

Step 3.   Work with a partner. Say your number 2. Your partner should say the correct comparative and superlative forms without looking at the book. If his or her answer is correct, say, "That's right." If it's not correct, say, "No, try again."

Step 4.   Then your partner says his or her number 2, and you give the correct comparative and superlative forms. Take turns doing this.

1. fast faster the fastest	2.	3.	4.	5.
6.	7.	8:	9.	10.
11.	12.	13.	14.	15.

Adjectives and Adverbs

modern	expensive	nice	comfortable	sharp	dull
slowly	serious	quickly	fast	bad	far
careful	strong	quiet	noisy	dangerous	interesting
exciting	cheap	good	badly	late	high
tired	warm	deep	salty	delicious	crunchy
smooth	heavy	intelligent	crowded	friendly	early

Exercise 9.   Multiple Choice. Circle the letter of the correct answer.

1. "None of the boys wants to work."

    "That is true, but Paul and Joseph are certainly _____."

    (A) more lazy   (C) the most lazy

    (B) lazy   (D) the laziest

2. Chris is the _____ student in the class.

    (A) better   (C) the best

    (B) better than   (D) most good

3. Peter didn't eat breakfast today, so of course he is _____ than we are.

    (A) more hungry   (C) hungry

    (B) hungrier   (D) the hungriest

4. She is _____ than her sister.

    (A) taller   (C) more tall

    (B) gooder   (D) more good

5. "Let's buy this cake."

    "Good idea. It looks much _____ than the other one."

    (A) fresher and deliciouser   (C) more fresh and deliciouser

    (B) fresher and more delicious   (D) more fresh and more delicious

6. "Of all the students in our class, who speaks English _____?"

    "Several students speak English well, but Carrine's English is the nicest."

    (A) the good   (C) the best

    (B) good   (D) better

7. "Which do you think is _____ for an English speaker to learn—Arabic or Chinese?"

    "The answer is definitely Chinese. The writing and pronunciation are extremely hard."

    (A) more hard   (C) the most hard

    (B) more difficult   (D) the most difficult

8. "Let's take a walk in the park today."

    "Are you kidding? It's too _____ to go outside today!"

    (A) the coldest   (C) colder

    (B) more cold   (D) cold

Exercise 10.   Review Test

Part 1.   Read this short passage. Underline the correct words.

Next year three friends and I are going to take a trip together. That was an easy

decision. But now we have a (more hard, harder) decision. We have to choose a place. Our

three choices are Hawaii, Russia, and Argentina. The ticket to Hawaii is expensive, but the ticket to Argentina is (expensiver, more expensive) than the ticket to Hawaii. However, the ticket to Russia is (more expensive, the most expensive) of all three places.

Argentina has good weather in the summer, but I think the weather in Russia in the summer is (gooder, better). Some people in our group think that the weather in Hawaii is (better, the best) of all three places.

What are we going to do? I think that Russia is (nicer, more nice) than Hawaii, but some other people don't agree. Greg thinks that Argentina is (interestinger, more interesting) than Hawaii, but he wants to visit Russia, too.

Part 2. Read this short passage. There are four mistakes. Circle the mistakes and write the correct forms above the mistake.

Last week I read a book called *Victory*. It was very interesting. However, I just finished reading a book called *Behind the Wall*. I think this book was most interesting than *Victory*. Both books are about the war in the early 1900s, but *Behind the Wall* was more better.

Some people don't want to read *Behind the Wall* because it's so long. *Victory* was a long book. It has 350 pages, but *Behind the Wall* is longer from *Victory*. *Behind the Wall* has 468 pages.

I also enjoyed *Behind the Wall* because it is more easy to read. The author wrote very clearly. Some parts of *Behind the Wall* were difficult to understand, but this was not true with *Victory*.

Part 3. Read each sentence carefully. Look at the underlined part. If it is correct, circle the word *correct*. If it is wrong, circle the wrong part and write the correct form above.

correct   wrong   1. Alaska is the <u>largest</u> state in the United States.

correct   wrong   2. Which car is <u>the cheapest</u>?

correct   wrong   3. Of all the people in your class, who speaks <u>the most quickly</u>?

correct   wrong   4. It's wrong to say that the Statue of Liberty is <u>taller from</u> the
                        Eiffel Tower.

correct   wrong   5. Do you know the name of <u>brightest</u> star in the sky?

correct   wrong   6. The smell of onions is <u>more stronger than</u> the smell of oranges.

Unit 11

Modals

1. *might*   4. *could*   7. *should*
2. *may*   5. *will*   8. *had better*
3. *can*   6. *would*   9. *must*

In this unit, we will study about a special group of words called modals. Modals change the meaning of a sentence. They give the sentence a special "flavor" or "direction." Each modal has a different meaning and is used at different times. Modals are difficult for some students because some modals have more than one meaning. Study these general notes about modals. Then study the information on each of the modals.

Modals

1. Here are some modals with some of their meanings.

might	possibility
may	(1) possibility (2) permission
can	(1) ability (2) permission
could	(1) polite request (2) past ability (3) suggestion (4) conditional
will	(1) future (2) nice request
would	(1) offering/inviting (2) polite request (3) conditional
should	(1) advising/suggesting (2) expectation
had better	strong advice or warning
must	(1) obligation/necessity (2) conclusion

2. Modals are found between the subject and the verb.

   <u>Sue and Lim</u> **can** <u>play</u> tennis very well.
         s   v

   <u>You</u> **had better** <u>clean</u> up your room right now.
    s   v

   <u>It</u> **must** <u>be</u> about 9:30 now.
    s   v

3. Modals never have any special ending such as **s, ed,** or **ing.**

   John play<u>s</u> soccer well.   John can **play** soccer well.
   Linda watch<u>ed</u> TV six hours.   Linda must **like** TV a lot.
   Karen is work<u>ing</u> now.   Karen should **finish** soon.

4. When two verbs are together in a sentence, sometimes we find the word **to** between them. However, we do not use **to** between a modal and a verb.

   I **want** to **go** to the store now.   I **will go** to the store now.
   You **like** to **study** with friends.   Perhaps you **should study** alone.

5. The negative forms of modals are very easy. You can always add **not.** Some modals also have a contraction form. (Be careful! Some modals do not have contraction forms.)

Modal	Negative	Negative Contraction
might	might not	——
may	may not	——
can	can not OR cannot	can't
could	could not	couldn't
will	will not	won't
would	would not	wouldn't
should	should not	shouldn't
had better	had better not	——
must	must not	mustn't

6. Making questions with modals is very easy. We just move the modal before the subject. This is similar to questions with the verb **be.**

   She <u>can play</u> tennis.   <u>Can</u> she <u>play</u> tennis?
   They <u>will be</u> late.   <u>Will</u> they <u>be</u> late?
   We <u>could go</u> to Italy for vacation.   Where <u>could</u> we <u>go</u> for vacation?
   You <u>would like</u> some tea to drink.   What <u>would</u> you <u>like</u> to drink?

CAREFUL! Watch out for these common mistakes.

1. Do not use **to** after single-word modals.
   - wrong: Andrea should to study more.
   - correct: Andrea should study more.

2. Do not add any endings (**s, ed,** or **ing**) to verbs after modals.
   - wrong: Shawn will helps Jim with the work.
   - correct: Shawn will help Jim with the work.

3. Do not use **don't, doesn't,** or **didn't** to make negative forms of modals.
   - wrong: Kathy doesn't can speak Japanese well.
   - correct: Kathy can't speak Japanese well.

4. Do not use **do, does,** or **did** in a question with a modal.
   - wrong: Do you could help me with this homework?
   - correct: Could you help me with this homework?

Might — Meaning: Possible, Maybe, Perhaps

examples:
- A: What time is it now? I don't have my watch.
- B: I'm not sure. It **might** be around 8:30. Does that sound right to you?

- A: I called Sue's house, but no one answered the phone. I wonder where she is.
- B: Well, she **might** be at the office. Why don't you call there?

Exercise 1.   Read the situations and then read the three sentences. Which of the sentences might be true? Write the letter of the correct answer on the line. Follow the example.

example: Jack has a small vegetable garden. He worked in the garden from 2 to 6. It was a very hot day. It's 6:15 now. Jack might _A, C_ .

(A) be very tired   (B) be very rich
(C) have tomatoes in his garden.

(*Explanation:* If Jack worked in the hot sun for four hours, it is possible that (A) he is very tired. Jack has a vegetable garden, so (C) is also possible because many people who have vegetable gardens have tomatoes. However, (B) is not correct here. We have no reason to think that Jack is a rich person.)

1. Vicki is going to go on vacation on Saturday. She finishes work at 5. Today is Friday, and the time now is 6. Vicki might be _____.

(A) at the office   (B) at home   (C) on an airplane

2. Linda likes sweets. She is at the store right now. She might _____.

(A) buy a cake   (B) buy a steak   (C) be a child

3. Sami speaks Arabic. He is from northern Africa. He might be from _____.

(A) Saudi Arabia   (B) Morocco   (C) Kuwait

4. Victor lives in a large city in Canada. He might _____.

(A) live in Toronto   (B) live in Seattle   (C) ride a bus to work

5. Peter has a Japanese car. His car might be a _____.

(A) Honda   (B) Toyota   (C) Nissan

May — Meaning 1: Possible, Maybe, Perhaps

examples: A: I wonder where Tom is.
                B: I'm not sure. He **may** be at home or he **may** be at school.

Note: For this usage, **may** and **might** have the same meaning.

───

Exercise 2.   Match the situation on the left with the possible reason or cause on the right by drawing a line between the two that go together best. Follow the example.

Group 1

1. I can't go with you to the movie tonight   because the teacher may give a pop test.

2. Don't touch that spider   if I'm not feeling tired.

3. I stayed up late to study   because I may have to work tomorrow.

4. I may go to Rick's party tonight   because it may be poisonous.

Group 2

5. I don't think we can play tennis today   if this headache doesn't stop soon.

6. I may go to the doctor's later   because I don't like my boss.

7. I am studying French   because it may rain.

8. I may quit my job soon   because I may get a job in France.

May — Meaning 2: Permission

A: Brenda, **may** I ask you a question?
B: Sure. Go ahead.
A: Why did you quit working at the bank?

Note: In this case, **may** is similar to **can.** In conversation, it is OK to use **can** to ask permission to do something. However, in formal language, we usually use **may.**

Exercise 3.   Unscramble the words to make a permission sentence with *may*.
Write your new sentence on the line. Pay attention to punctuation
(. or *?*). Follow the example.

example: [?] help may you I
        A: <u>May I help you?</u>
        B: Yes, I'd like a hamburger, french fries, and a large soft
               drink.

1. [?] here sit may I

    A: _____

    B: Sure. No one's sitting there.

2. [.] books if three you you card may library have out a check

    A: Hi, I'm a new student here, and I'd like to check out some books.

    B: _____

3. [?] take we photographs may here

    A: _____

    B: Yes, but don't use flash.

4. [?] I your use telephone to may my mom call

    A: _____

    B: Sure. Go ahead. It's on the table near the television.

5. [.] send an to computer if you e-mail you use this may want message to her

    A: I need to get in touch with my professor right away.

    B: _____

Can — Meaning 1: Ability

example: *A:* **Can** you speak any foreign languages?
               B: I **can** speak French. I **can** read German, but I **can't** speak it very well.

Note: When **can** means "ability," it has the same meaning as the expression **be able to.**

examples: I **can** speak French. = I am able to speak French.
             They **can** swim well. = They are able to swim well.

Exercise 4.   Complete the sentences with the correct forms. In the first sentence, use *be able to* and in the second sentence *can*. Follow the example.

      example: John isn't able to write Arabic. = John <u> can't write </u> Arabic.

1. The flowers _____ grow here because there is not enough sun-

   light.

   = The flowers can't grow here because there is not enough sunlight.

2. They _____ send e-mail.

   = They can't send e-mail.

3. Carol and Sue are able to speak French well.

   = Carol and Sue _____ French well.

4. Most people are able to cook spaghetti, but they _____ bake

   bread.

   = Most people _____ cook spaghetti, but they can't bake bread.

5. She's only twelve, so of course she is not able to drive a car yet.

   = She's only twelve, so of course she _____ a car yet.

Speaking Activity

Exercise 5. Speaking Activity: What can you do? Work with a partner.

Step 1. The left column is your list. There are eighteen actions. Put a check mark (√) by five of the actions. Do not let anyone see your list. You can choose actions that you really can do, and you can choose actions that you cannot do. You do not have to tell the truth.

Step 2. Work with a partner. Take turns trying to guess each other's list. Student A begins by asking any of the actions. For example, "Can you bake a pineapple cake?" If Student B has a check mark by that action, then B says "Yes, I can," and it is still student A's turn to ask questions. When B says "No, I can't" to a question, then it is B's turn to ask a question.

Step 3. The winner is the first student to guess all five of his or her partner's actions.

Your List	*Your Partner's List*
1. ___ play tennis	1. ___ play tennis
2. ___ speak French	2. ___ speak French
3. ___ fly a plane	3. ___ fly a plane
4. ___ run 100 meters in 10 seconds	4. ___ run 100 meters in 10 seconds
5. ___ drive a race car	5. ___ drive a race car
6. ___ ski down a really high mountain	6. ___ ski down a really high mountain
7. ___ understand science well	7. ___ understand science well
8. ___ sing high and low notes	8. ___ sing high and low notes
9. ___ say the alphabet backward	9. ___ say the alphabet backward
10. ___ bake a pineapple cake	10. ___ bake a pineapple cake
11. ___ eat really spicy food	11. ___ eat really spicy food
12. ___ read Japanese	12. ___ read Japanese
13. ___ add and subtract quickly	13. ___ add and subtract quickly
14. ___ operate a computer	14. ___ operate a computer
15. ___ rollerblade	15. ___ rollerblade
16. ___ write with your left hand	16. ___ write with your left hand
17. ___ drink coffee without milk or sugar	17. ___ drink coffee without milk or sugar
18. ___ cook rice	18. ___ cook rice

Speaking Activity

Exercise 6.   Speaking Activity: Who can do what?

Step 1. Below is a list of eight names and eight activities. In the area marked "Your List," write the eight names in the first blank. Mix up the names. In the second blank, write the actions. Mix these up as well. When you finish, you will have eight original sentences (such as "Maria can swim well.")

Step 2. Work with a partner. Take turns asking *yes-no* questions to guess your partner's sentences. For example, ask "Can Ann play tennis?" If that is your partner's sentence, he or she will answer "Yes, she can," and then you should write that sentence in the column "Your Partner's List."
If the answer is "No she can't," then the turn passes to your partner. The winner is the first student who can guess all eight of the other student's sentences.

Names	*Actions*
Ann	play tennis
Linda	play the piano
Danny	read Arabic
Maria	fly a plane
Dan	write Chinese
Fran	swim well
Tom	cook meat loaf
Sammy	type fast

Your List

1. _____ can _____
2. _____ can _____
3. _____ can _____
4. _____ can _____
5. _____ can _____
6. _____ can _____
7. _____ can _____
8. _____ can _____

Your Partner's List

1. _____ can _____
2. _____ can _____
3. _____ can _____
4. _____ can _____
5. _____ can _____
6. _____ can _____
7. _____ can _____
8. _____ can _____

Can — Meaning 2: Permission

A: Brenda, **can** I ask you a question?
B: Sure. Go ahead.
A: Why did you quit working at the bank?

Note: In conversation, it is OK to use **can** to ask permission to do something. However, in formal language, we usually use **may.** See the information on **may** for an example of this.

Exercise 7. This exercise has six small conversations in it. Some conversations use *can* to ask permission, and others use *can* to express ability. Read speaker 1's comment on the left and then find what speaker 2 probably says in response. Write the letter of speaker 2's response on the lines on the left. Follow the example.

Speaker 1

<u>D</u> 1. Can Michael drive?

_____ 2. Can Michael drive your car?

_____ 3. Can I sit here?

_____ 4. Hey, can you go with us to the beach tomorrow?

_____ 5. Excuse me. Can I use your telephone?

_____ 6. Can you operate this computer? It looks kind of hard.

_____ 7. Can I borrow five dollars until the day after tomorrow?

_____ 8. Can elementary school students have beepers at school?

Speaker 2

A: No way! My insurance only covers me.

B: I know it looks hard, but actually, it's pretty easy. Let me show you.

C: Actually, I'm saving this seat for my friend. Sorry.

D: Yes, he can. He has a license. He knows how to drive well.

E: I'm really sorry, but I'm broke.

F: No, my father said that I have to stay home and help clean the house.

G: A long time ago schools made rules against that. Young children don't have any need for them.

H: Let me ask my supervisor. If she says no, there is another one down the hall.

CHALLENGE A student says that his English-speaking friends never say, "May I use your pen?" They always say "Can I use your pen?" You are the teacher. Can you explain this?

Could — Meaning 1: Polite Request

examples: A: **Could** you tell me the time, please?
              B: Sure. It's 11:20.

              A: Excuse me. **Could** I borrow your pen for a minute?
              B: Of course. Here you go.

Exercise 8.   Scrambled Conversations

Part 1.   Unscramble the words to make a request with *could*. Write your new
            question on the line. Pay attention to punctuation *[?]*. Follow the example.

(A)   [?] me museum the of location you please tell the could

    Could you please tell me the location of the museum?

(B)   [?] salad and please glass of could you a me a iced tea bring

_____

(C)   [?] in front of you this bag during takeoff put you under the seat could please

_____

(D)   [?] could again please word you explain that

_____

(E)   [?] forty-cent give me please you five stamps could

_____

(F)   [?] please watch could price tell me you the of this

_____

(G)   [?] window you open could please the

_____

Part 2. Match the polite requests that you just wrote above to the conversations below by writing the letter of the request by the number of the conversation. The first one has been done for you.

1. _____ OK, let me see. The sale price for this month only is $49.95.

2. _____ Sure. Would you like lemon with your tea?

3. _____ I already tried, but I can't. I think it's stuck.

4. _____ OK. A dilemma is a kind of problem. It's a situation when you don't really know what to do. For example, if you like your current job a lot but another company offers you more money, do you change jobs? Part of you wants to stay, and part of you wants to leave. This is a dilemma. Is that clear now?

5. _____ I already have another bag there. Could you put this in the overhead compartment?

6. _A_ Go to the corner and turn left. Go two blocks. It will be on your right.

7. _____ Here you go. That will be two dollars.

Could — Meaning 2: Past Ability, Past Tense of *Can*

A: What does this French word mean in English?
B: I'm sorry, but I don't know. When I was a child, I **could** speak French well because my family lived in France, but now I can't even remember how to say "How are you?" in French.

A: Grandpa, how much did soft drinks cost when you were a kid?
B: When I was your age, we **could** buy a soft drink for ten cents.

Note: We only use **could** for the past of **can** when the action was over a period of time. *Careful:* We do NOT use **could** for past if it is a single past action in an affirmative sentence. In this case, we use **was able to** or **were able to**. In a negative sentence, we can use **couldn't** or **wasn't** or **weren't able to**.

examples: *A:* Did you find your keys?
B: Yes, I **was** finally **able to** find them. They were under the sofa!
(NOT: Yes, I could find them.)
OR
B: No, I **wasn't able to** find them./No, I **couldn't** find them.
(Both are OK.)

If you are talking about a single, past action about ability:

was/were able to	yes
wasn't/weren't able to	yes
could	no (only for past repeated actions)
couldn't	yes

Exercise 9.   Correct or wrong? Read each sentence carefully. Look at the underlined part. If the underlined part is correct, circle the word *correct*. If
it is wrong, circle the wrong part and write the correct form above
the mistake.

correct   wrong   1.   *A:* Did you ever find your German-English dictionary?

                           B: Yes, I <u>found</u> it.

correct   wrong   2.   *A:* Did you ever find your German-English dictionary?

                           B: Yes, I <u>could find</u> it.

correct   wrong   3.   *A:* Did you ever find your German-English dictionary?

                           B: No, I <u>wasn't able to find</u> it.

correct   wrong   4.   *A:* Did you ever find your German-English dictionary?

                           B: No, I <u>couldn't find</u> it.

correct   wrong   5.   *A:* Did you talk to Martha last night?

                           B: No. I called and called, but I <u>couldn't reach</u> her.

correct   wrong   6.   *A:* Did you talk to Martha last night?

                           B: Yes, finally I <u>could talk</u> to her at 11:30.

correct   wrong   7.   *A:* Did you pass your driving test yesterday?

                           B: No, I <u>wasn't able to pass</u> it. I might try again next week.

correct   wrong   8.   *A:* Were you able to get your driver's license yesterday?

                           B: No, I <u>couldn't get</u> it. I have to try again.

correct   wrong   9.   *A:* How was Mr. Crawford's speech at the meeting?

                           B: It was great. He <u>could give</u> a really wonderful speech!

correct   wrong   10.   *A:* Where is Carolyn?

                           B: Finally she <u>could get</u> her visa for Russia, so she's at the

                                 travel agency now making flight and hotel reservations.

Could — Meaning 3: Suggesting

examples: *A:*   Where do you want to eat dinner?

B: We **could** go to Pizza House. How's that sound to you?

A: My friends are going on a trip to Alaska, but I can't go with them because I don't have enough money for the ticket and the hotels.

B: Well, you have five months until the trip, right? You **could** get a part-time job at the library or at the store.

Exercise 10.   Read these situations and then write a suggestion for the person using *could.* When you have finished, check your possible answers in small groups. Who has the most interesting suggestion? The best suggestion? The funniest suggestion? Follow the example.

example: *Problem:* "I don't know what to do. My aunt gave me a new CD, but I already have this same CD. On the one she gave me, she wrote "Happy Birthday" with a black pen, so I can't return this CD to the store."

Suggestion: <u>You could sell your first CD at a used CD</u>
    <u>store.</u>

1.   *Problem:* "There is a big dinner party tomorrow night at a good friend's house. I'm sure she will serve meat for the main course, and many of the side dishes will have a cream sauce or some kind of animal product such as butter. I'm a vegetarian. I don't know what to do."

Suggestion: _____

_____

2.   *Problem:* "My son is not doing so well in school. He was a very good student, but recently his grades haven't been very good. I don't want to put a lot of pressure on him. Any suggestions?"

Suggestion: _____

_____

3. *Problem:* "I have a big test next Monday, but I don't really understand the material

    that is going to be on the test. I have tried to read the book, but I just don't under-

    stand it."

    Suggestion: _____

    _____

4. *Problem:* "It's my aunt's birthday, but I don't know what to get her. I like her a lot,

    and I want to get a very special gift for her, but I just don't have any ideas for a

    present. The last time I saw my aunt in person was back in 1989, so I don't really

    know her so well."

    Suggestion: _____

    _____

5. *Problem:* "I need some change to make a phone call. I have a one-dollar bill but no

    coins. What are my possibilities?"

    Suggestion: _____

    _____

Could — Meaning 4: Conditional Idea/*If*

examples: A: Where do you want to eat dinner?
              B: Well, if I had one hundred dollars, we **could** eat at that expensive steak
                   place on the bay.

              A: What's wrong?
              B: I can't do my homework because I can't find my black pen. We have to
                   use a black pen for this assignment. If I had a black pen, I **could** finish
                   this in twenty minutes.

Note: This meaning is a little difficult. It is not for beginning students. The usual pattern
here is **if + SUBJECT + PAST TENSE,** then **SUBJECT + could + VERB.**

examples: If I <u>had</u> a million dollars, I <u>could quit</u> my job and stay home forever.
              If you <u>studied</u> more, you <u>could pass</u> the English exam easily.
              If we <u>practiced</u> tennis more, we <u>could be</u> really good players.

Exercise 11. Read each situation and then write an *if* sentence with *could*. Follow the examples.

examples: I'm in the bank. I can't go to my car because it's raining really hard. I don't have an umbrella. I need to get home quickly.
If I had an umbrella, I could go to my car now.
This sign says something in big red letters. It's written in Spanish. I can't read it because I don't know Spanish.
If I knew Spanish, I could read the sign.

1. I'm flying to New York. The morning flight is only $80, and my flight is $150. I want to save $70, but I can't leave so early.

   _____

2. The weather outside is beautiful. I would like to go to the park. I don't have a car or a bicycle.

   _____

3. I don't know the past tense of ride. I don't have a dictionary, so I can't look it up.

   _____

4. I want to call Victor, but he doesn't have a phone.

   _____

5. This food is so salty. I can't eat it.

   _____

Will — Meaning 1: Future Time

example: A: It might rain tomorrow. What **will** you do if it rains?
B: I'm not sure. If it rains, I think **I'll** go to the library.

Note: Use **be** + **going to** (not **will**) to talk about a future event that you have already planned.

examples: A: What **are** you **going to** do tomorrow? I need someone to help me with this homework.
B: Sorry, but I can't help you. **I'm going to** visit my aunt. She's in the hospital. (Wrong: I'll visit my aunt.)

A: We**'re going to** go to the beach tomorrow. Do you want to go with us?
B: I'd like to go, but I can't. My brother and I **are going to** shop for a gift for our father's birthday. (Wrong: My brother and I will shop . . . .)

Note: Use **will** if you decide to do something at the same time you speak.

examples: *A:*   Oh, no! I don't have any more salt, and I'm still making food for the party.

   B: Don't worry! **I'll** go to the store to get some more. (Wrong: I'm going to go . . . .)

   A: Thanks! I have so many things to do to get ready. I really appreciate it.

   A: How much are apples? I only need eight.

   B: They're forty cents each, or you can get a dozen for four dollars.

   A: OK, then **I'll** take a dozen. Maybe **I'll** give the extra four to my sister. (Wrong: I'm going to take . . . .)

Exercise 12.   Fill in the blanks with *will* or *be going to*. Sometimes both are possible.

1. *A:* What _____ do next Saturday?

   B: Gosh, I don't know. Why?

2. *A:* Oh, no! No one brought ice. That's the end of this party!

   B: Don't worry. Listen. I have an idea. I have a car, so I

   _____ go to the store to get some ice.

3. *A:* Do you think Luke _____ get that job in

   Boston?

   B: I don't know. I hope he gets it.

4. *A:* Frank, I _____ go to the post office. Do you

   have anything to be mailed?

   B: No, but thanks for asking.

5. *A:* Brenda, can you take me to the bank now? I need to cash

   this check.

   B: Sure. I _____ drive you

   there.

6. *A:* Why do you have that suitcase with you?

   B: Because I _____ fly to Los Angeles when school

   finishes today.

7. *A:* Wow, this box is heavy!

   B: Don't lift that by yourself. I _____ help you with it.

8. *A:* I saw Jan this morning. She has her driving test today.

   B: Yes, I saw her, too. She was a little nervous, but I think she

   _____ pass the test this time!

9. *A:* Excuse me.

   B: Yes, I _____ be with you in a minute. Let me

   make one more phone call, OK?

10. *A:* Gosh, it's so hot in here! Could you please open that window?

    B: Sure. I _____ do it.

Will — Meaning 2: Asking Someone to Do Something

examples: *A:*   **Will** you help me with these packages? They're sort of heavy.
            B: Sure. No sweat.

Exercise 13.   When people make a request with *will,* they often add a second sentence to explain why they are making the request. In the above example, the explanation sentence is "They're sort of heavy." Draw a line to connect the *will* requests with the correct explanations. Follow the example.

1. Will you pass me the salt?   I can't answer it myself.

2. Will you tell me the time?   I wonder if it needs more salt.

3. Will you help me with this question? I can't reach it.

4. Will you taste this soup?   I forgot my watch today.

5. Will you turn up the volume?   I'd like to call you up.

6. Will you open your books to page 200? Time is up.

7. Will you be home later?   I can't hear it very well.

8. Will you please pass in your papers? I'd like to talk about the chart on

                                          this page.

Would — Meaning 1: Offering or Inviting
(Would you like . . . ?)

examples: A: **Would** you **like** some coffee or tea?
           B: I'll have coffee, please.
           A: What **would** you **like** in your coffee? Cream? Sugar?
           B: Just a little sugar.

           A: What **would** you **like** to do now?
           B: We could go to a movie. Let's go see that new James Bond movie.

Note: **Would you like** is a polite way of asking **do you want.**

Exercise 14. Complete the sentences with the correct forms. In the first sentence, use *want* and in the second sentence *would like.* Follow the examples.

examples: (want)   _Do_____ you _want_ to play tennis this evening?
           (would like) _Would_ you _like_ to play tennis this evening?

           (want)   John _doesn't want_____ any cookies now.
           (would like) John _wouldn't like_____ any cookies now.

           (*Note:* We have to use a negative because of the word *any.*)

1. (want)   Where _____ Pedro _____ to go on vacation?

    (would like) Where _____ Pedro _____ to go on vacation?

2. (want)   I _____ some coffee with cream.

    (would like) I _____ some coffee with cream.

3. (want)   They _____ some help with the homework.

    (would like) They _____ some help with the homework.

4. (want)   _____ you _____ to watch TV with us?

    (would like) _____ you _____ to watch TV with us?

5. (want)   Why _____ you _____ to stay at that hotel? It's not

                  very good.

    (would like) Why _____ you _____ to stay at that hotel? It's not

                  very good.

6. (want)   _____ you _____ a sandwich? We have several differ-

                  ent kinds of meat.

(would like) _____ you _____ a sandwich? We have several differ-

ent kinds of meat.

7. (want) I _____ another sandwich, please. They are

really great!

(would like) I _____ another sandwich, please. They are

really great!

8. (want) _____ the teacher _____ us to type our reports?

(would like) _____ the teacher _____ us to type our reports?

Would — Meaning 2: Polite Request

examples: A: Jill, my car is at the repair place now. When we finish work this afternoon, **would** you drive me there so I can pick up my car?
B: Sure, but I can't leave here till five o'clock.
A: No problem. The repair place is open until six.

A: **Would** you read this letter and tell me how it sounds to you?
B: I'd be glad to. What is the purpose of this letter?
A: I'm writing to complain about a problem I had with a clerk at their store.

Exercise 15. What kinds of requests do different people make? Read the description of the people in the conversation. Then write two possible requests with *would* for each person. When you finish, compare your answers with other students'. Follow the example.

example: A dentist is speaking to a patient.
(A) _Would you please sit here?_
(B) _Would you open your mouth?_

1. A teacher is talking to the students in his or her class.

(A) _____

(B) _____

2. A customer is talking to a taxi driver.

    (A) _____

    (B) _____

3. Mary is speaking to her friend Julia. Julia is at the front door of Mary's house. Julia is

    visiting Mary.

    (A) _____

    (B) _____

4. Paul and Ben are making plans for the weekend. Saturday is Ben's birthday.

    (A) _____

    (B) _____

5. Mike and Anna are in the same English class. They have a huge test on Monday.

    Mike is worried about his grade on the test.

    (A) _____

    (B) _____

Would — Meaning 3: Conditional Sentences with *If*

examples: *A:*   If you received a hundred dollars from your father, what **would** you do?
              B: I don't know. I think I **would** buy some new CDs.

Note: The last sentence means "I think I would buy some new CDs if I received a hundred dollars." It is not necessary to say the **if** information because it is understood by everyone in the conversation.

              A: I can't understand this letter. It's written in Greek.
              B: **I'd** help you if I knew Greek, but I don't know a word.

Note: This meaning is a little difficult. It is not for beginning students. The usual pattern here is **if** + **SUBJECT** + **PAST TENSE,** then **SUBJECT** + **would** + **VERB.** You can put the **if** part first or second; it doesn't matter. We don't use present tense with the **if** part. We always use a past tense verb, but we are talking about a present time situation.

examples: If I <u>had</u> a million dollars, I <u>would quit</u> my job and stay home forever.
(I don't have a million dollars now, but if I **had** a million dollars **now,** I would quit my job and stay home forever. Note the use of **had** with a present time situation.)

If we <u>practiced</u> tennis more, we <u>would be</u> really good players.
(We don't practice enough every day, so we are not very good players. Look at the verb in the phrase **if we practiced.** It is a past tense verb, but we are talking about a present time situation.)

Exercise 16.   Write original answers for the *if* questions in numbers 1–8. Then add two original questions for numbers 9 and 10 followed by your own answers. Then take turns asking the other students in the class the questions. Are the other students' answers the same as yours? Are there any surprises? Follow the examples. Exchange books with a classmate to check the grammar of the questions.

examples: If you had a headache, what would you do?
_____If I had a headache, I would take two aspirins._____
What would your mother do if you came home late?
_____My mother would get angry if I came home late._____

1. If you had a chance to go to one city in Europe, which city would you visit?

    _____

2. If you could meet anyone in the world (dead or alive), who would you meet?

    _____

3. What would your teacher do if you copied your friend's homework?

    _____

4. If you had $1,000 right now, what would you buy?

    _____

5. If your family gave you a new car, what kind of car would you ask for?

    _____

6. What would you do if you found a small insect in your salad at a restaurant?

    _____

7. What would you do if you found a small insect in your salad at a friend's house?

   _____

8. If you ate a quart (liter) of ice cream every day, what would happen?

   _____

9. _____

   _____?

   _____

10. _____

    _____?

    _____

    _____

Should — Meaning 1: Advice or Suggestion; It's a Good Idea

examples: A: Well, which shirt **should** I get? The red one or the blue one?

              B: The red one looks nice, but it costs $40. The blue one is OK, and it's only $30. I think you **should**★ get the blue one.

              A: Did you call the bank about that job?

              B: No, I decided not to do that.

              A: Why?

              B: I don't have the right skills for the job. I'd never get it.

              A: What? Are you joking? You can type, you have basic computer skills, and you're great with people. You're just the right person for that job. I really think you **should** call the bank and set up an interview as soon as possible.

★ Using only *should* is not common. We usually say "I think" when we use *should*. *Example:* I think you should talk to him. OR I don't think you should do that.

Exercise 17. Read the situations and write a sentence in which you give some advice to the person with a problem. Follow the example. (Remember that we usually say "I think" when we use *should*.)

example: Susan got a divorce only three weeks ago. She has met a nice man and is thinking about getting married to him in the near future. What should she do?

I think she should wait until she knows him better.

1. Mr. Findley is a math teacher. Two of his students were cheating on the last test. Gina gave some answers to Peter. What should Mr. Findley do?

   _____

2. Irene works very hard. She is often very tired because she works so much. She never takes a vacation, and she always stays at the office very long hours. What do you think about her situation?

   _____

3. Officer Johnston stopped a driver for speeding. The driver said that the reason he was speeding was that he was late for a very important meeting. What should Officer Johnston do?

   _____

4. Linda is going to have six friends come to her house for dinner. Three of her friends are vegetarian, but the other three like meat. The vegetarians will not be happy if there is any meat on the table, but the other three are accustomed to eating meat. What should Linda do?

   _____

5. I have a good job. I get along well with my coworkers. Yesterday I saw a job at a nearby company for the same job that I am doing now. The salary at the other job is about thirty percent more than I currently make. I wonder if I should apply for this other job. What do you think I should do?

   _____

Should — Meaning 2: Expectation about Something

examples: A: Wait a minute. Something is wrong.

B: What do you mean?

A: Here, count these cards. We **should** have fifty-two, but there are only fifty.

A: Wow, isn't this weather great today?

B: Yes, it is. I can't believe it's August and we're having such great weather.

A: It is great, isn't it? Really, the weather **should** be much hotter in August.

Special Note about *Should* and *Ought To*

Should and **ought to** have the same meaning. Remember that **ought to** uses **to,** but **should** never does.

examples:

Meaning 1:	You **should** take some aspirin.	=	You **ought to** take some aspirin.
	I **should** study more.	=	I **ought to** study more.
Meaning 2:	The bus **should** arrive soon.	=	The bus **ought to** arrive soon.
	It's 5:30, so he **should** be home.	=	It's 5:30, so he **ought to** be home.

Exercise 18.   Read these strange or unusual situations. Tell what the problem is by telling how the situation should be. Use *should* or *ought to*. (They have the same meaning.) Follow the example.

example: A: I just called Jill, but she wasn't home.

B: That's strange. It's 8:30, so she <u>should be home now.</u>
<u>(OR ought to be home now.)</u>   .

1. A: This spaghetti is still hard.

B: That's strange. I cooked it for fifteen minutes, so

_____

_____.

2. A: Oh, no. This check is wrong.

B: What do you mean?

A: It's only for one week of work, but I worked for two weeks, so

_____

_____.

3. *A:* Hey, this box of crayons only has nine crayons.

   B: Wow, you're right. One is missing. The box _____

   _____.

4. *A:* I think the teacher made a mistake with my grade.

   B: What do you mean?

   A: Well, the test has one hundred questions, and I missed nineteen, but the teacher

   wrote seventy-one on my test.

   B: Yeah, that's wrong. Your score _____

   _____.

5. *A:* Can you believe this weather? I can't believe how hot it is!

   B: The weather forecaster on TV said that the weather is warmer than usual now.

   A: I heard that, too. Today's high temperature will be ninety-two, but this is

   extremely unusual for this area of Canada for September.

   B: Yeah, the weather

   _____.

Had Better — Meaning: Strong Advice or Suggestion with a Warning

examples: *A:*   My finger is still bleeding.
   B: I think you**'d** better go to the doctor now. You might need some stitches.

   A: What time is it?
   B: It's almost seven.
   A: Oh, no! I**'d** better leave now, or I might miss the bus. See you later, Tim!

Note: **Had better** is similar to **should,** but it is stronger. It always has the idea that there is a penalty or consequence if the action does not happen. Be careful with this expression. It is always used by a person of higher authority to a person of lower authority. It may also be used between people of similar authority. It is very rude for a person of lower authority to use **had better** to a person of higher authority. For example, a child never uses **had better** to a parent, but a parent can use **had better** to a child.

Exercise 19. Draw a line from the sentences in the left column to the matching sentences in the right column to make a good conversation. Follow the example.

1. *Driver:* I don't have to show you my license. Why are you bothering me?

2. *Husband:* Do you think two chickens will be enough? Henry and Abby can really eat a lot.

3. *Friend 1:* OK, I'll see you at the party tonight, and I'll have ten bags of ice with me.

4. *Student:* I wrote this paper myself.

5. *Clerk:* This steak is cooked. Look. If you cut it, there is no pink part.

6. *Child:* I don't want to eat any more.

Parent: You'd better clean your plate,★ or you can't have any dessert.

Teacher: I know that you didn't write this. These are not your own words. You'd better tell me the truth, or I'll give you an F for sure.

Police Officer: Sir, you had better show me your license now. You were speeding. You were going fifty miles per hour, but the speed limit here is only thirty.

Customer: I don't want to argue. You'd better bring me another steak, or I'll ask to speak to the manager.

Wife: You're right. We'd better cook three chickens just to make sure we have enough food. Those two like to eat a lot!

Friend: OK, you'd better not forget, and you'd better not be late. We can't start the party without that ice!

★ clean your plate = eat all the food on your plate (conversational, informal language)

Must — Meaning 1: Obligation, Necessity (usually in formal written language)

example: A: What does that letter say?
  B: It says, "All students **must** register and pay for all classes before August 27."

  A: Can I get my driver's license now?
  B: How old are you?
  A: I'm fifteen.
  B: I'm afraid not. The rule book says that applicants **must** be at least sixteen.

A Special Note about *Must* and *Have To*

The meaning of obligation or necessity for **must** is the same as **have to.** There is one very important difference, however. In conversation, most North Americans do not use **must** to express necessity. In conversation or informal language, most people usually use **have to** to express obligation.

examples: A: Can I register for classes on August 30?
           B: No, everyone **has to** register before August 28.

             A: I want to get my driver's license now.
             B: How old are you?
             A: I'm fifteen.
             B: Sorry, you **have to** wait another year. You **have to** be sixteen to get a license.

Exercise 20.   Draw lines between the three parts to make complete sentences. Follow the example.

Group 1: Formal Situations

Canadians must	turn off their computers	in order to travel to Egypt.
Job applicants must	register for classes	in ink.
All passengers must	get a visa	before the plane can take off.
New students must	get a vaccination	by August 27.
All first graders must	sign their applications	against measles.

Group 2: Informal Situations

The teacher has to	eat vegetables and fruit	before we go to the movies.
I have to	finish this homework	because they are getting old.
Children have to	read that book twice	because she has an important meeting.
We have to	help my parents	so they can be strong and healthy.
You have to	end class a little early	in order to understand its message.

Speaking Activity

Exercise 21.   Speaking Activity: Things I Have to Do. Read each situation. Then make a list of five things you have to do in that situation. When you finish, compare your answers with a partner. Choose the best three answers that you and your partner can think of.

Situation A.   You are going to take a vacation in London. The month is November. You are going to be there for a week. You don't know anyone there. This is your first trip to London. This is also your first trip outside of the United States. What are five things that you have to do?

1. I _____.
2. I _____.
3. I _____.
4. I _____.
5. I _____.

Situation B.   You are going to have a dinner at your house. You want to invite about fifteen people. What are five things that you have to do?

1. I _____.
2. I _____.
3. I _____.
4. I _____.
5. I _____.

Situation C.   You are moving from your current place (house or apartment) to a new place. It is not very far (only about fifteen minutes by car). You want to move out on Friday and move in on Monday. What are five things that you have to do?

1. I _____.
2. I _____.
3. I _____.
4. I _____.
5. I _____.

A Special Note about the Negative Forms of *Must* and *Have To*

Must means the same as **have to.** The negative of **must** is **must not** (OR **mustn't**). The negative of **have to** is **don't have to** or **doesn't have to.** However, **must not** and **don't/doesn't have to** do NOT mean the same thing.

1. You **must** use a pencil for this test.   =   2. You **have to** use a pencil for this test.
1 and 2 have the same meaning: Do not use a pen or marker. Use only a pencil.

3. You **must not** use a pencil for this   ≠   4. You **don't have to** use a pencil for this
   test.   test.
Number 3 is the negative form for 1: Do not use a pencil. Use something else.
Number 4 is the negative form for 2: You can use a pencil if you want, but it is not necessary.

Exercise 22. Write *must not* or *doesn't/don't/didn't have to* and a verb on the lines. Follow the examples.

examples: *Teacher:* Here are the test papers. Mark all your answers on your answer sheet. You __must not use__ a pen or marker. A computer will check these papers, and the computer can only read pencil.
  Student: Mr. Bates, there is a line for our social security number. What should I do since I don't have a social security number?
  Teacher: We don't need that information, so you __don't have to write__ anything on that line. If you don't have a number, just leave it blank. If you know your number, please write it.

1. *Teacher:* Everyone in this class has to read one book and write a one-page summary of the book. I have a list of good books here. You _____ a book from this list. If you want, you can choose a book from the school library. However, you _____ a book without showing it to me first.
  Student: How long does the book have to be?
  Teacher: The book _____ less than two hundred pages.
  Student: Can we read a biography?
  Teacher: The book _____ fiction. Nonfiction is OK, too.

2. *Doctor:*   OK, Zack, here is your medicine. Take three of these pills every eight

hours.

Zack: Should I eat something before I take them?

Doctor: Food doesn't matter. You _____ eat anything first, but

you can if you want. However, you _____ any other

kinds of medicine while you are taking these pills. Mixing medicines is

dangerous.

Zack: When should I come back to see you again?

Doctor: Take all the pills first. The pills should be enough for about a week. If you

feel better, you _____ back again. If you suddenly feel

strange or very sick, you _____. (*Hint:* Use the verb

wait.) Come see me immediately.

Must — Meaning 2: Conclusion about a Situation

examples: A: I called John's home, but he's not there yet.
              B: Well, it's only 4:30, so he **must** be at school.

              A: Look at that new music store. It's so big!
              B: Wow! They **must** have a huge selection of CDs there.

Exercise 23.   Read the sentences below and then write a logical conclusion.
Follow the example.

                   example: *Clue 1:*   The new student's name is Pierre Rousseau.
                                Clue 2:   He speaks English with a French accent.
                                Question: What can you guess about Pierre's nationality?
                                               <u>He must be French.</u>

1. *Clue 1:*   Keith told you that his new Nissan car is parked in front of the school.

   Clue 2:   There are only two Japanese cars in the parking lot. The red one is a

Toyota, and the blue one is a Nissan.

   Question: What can you guess about the color of Keith's new car?

   _____

2. *Clue 1:*   Jack got up very early this morning. Then he worked at the office from 7:30 to 3:30.

     Clue 2:   He helped his neighbor paint her house from 4:30 to 5:45.

     Question: Jack told you yesterday that he might want to play tennis tonight. Jack just called to tell you that he cannot play tonight. Why do you think he can't play?

     _____

3. *Clue 1:*   Dan accidentally broke a vase at my house last night.

     Clue 2:   Dan just came to my house, and he has a small gift about fifteen inches high and twelve inches wide. The box is not very heavy.

     Question: What do you think is in the box?

     _____

4. *Clue 1:*   Brenda had a big exam yesterday in chemistry, which is her worst class.

     Clue 2:   She found out today that she made a 96 (out of 100) on the exam.

     Question: How do you think Brenda feels right now?

     _____

Exercise 24.   Multiple Choice. Circle the letter of the correct answer.

1. Where _____ you like to go tomorrow?

   (A) may   (C) had better

   (B) would   (D) can

2. The servant at the dinner party said, "Sir, _____ take your coat?"

   (A) would I   (C) may I

   (B) am I able to   (D) am I going to

3. I don't understand this word. _____ you explain it to me, please?

   (A) Might   (C) Will

   (B) Should   (D) May

4. Your temperature is 99.7. I think you _____ take some aspirin.

   (A) should   (C) are going to

   (B) would   (D) will

5. I turned the air conditioner on twenty minutes ago, but it's still hot in here. It

   _____ be cool in here already.

   (A) has to   (C) ought to

   (B) is going to   (D) would

6. Oh, no! The car broke down. I have my cellular phone, so I _____ call the car

   repair shop right now.

   (A) will   (C) am going to

   (B) must   (D) may

7. I bought all this paint because I _____ paint my house tomorrow.

   (A) will   (C) am going to

   (B) must   (D) would

8. There are many things that we _____ do on Saturday. One idea is to go to the

   beach. Another possibility is to visit the local art museum. You are my guest, so just

   tell me what you would like to do.

   (A) could   (C) would

   (B) must   (D) going to

Exercise 25.   Review Test

Part 1.   Underline the best modal in these sentences.

1. What (will you, would you, are you going to) do on Sunday?

2. I don't know if we can play tennis later. The weather report says that it (would, may, can) rain.

3. Jill needs to pass the big test tomorrow, so tonight she (can, might, has to) study hard.

4. I like this soup, but it (might, had better, must) be better if you add a little oregano.

5. This soup is awful. It (shouldn't, couldn't, wouldn't) have so much salt in it.

6. If you have time, you (are able to, ought to, are going to) read this book. It's so funny!

7. I am not wearing my watch today, but it (will, can, should) be around noon now.

8. All drivers (can, must, might) have their licenses with them when they drive.

Part 2.   Read each sentence carefully. Look at the underlined part. If the underlined part is correct, circle the word *correct*. If it is wrong, circle the wrong part and write the correct form above.

correct	wrong	1. The price tag on this radio says one dollar. The price <u>must be wrong</u>.
correct	wrong	2. It's noon. I <u>must meet</u> Jack for lunch now.
correct	wrong	3. Mommy and Daddy, you<u>'d better clean</u> the house now. It looks so dirty.
correct	wrong	4. Clerks at fast-food restaurants often say, "<u>May I help</u> you?"
correct	wrong	5. What? 60? You are a smart student, so your score <u>should be</u> much higher!
correct	wrong	6. If I had some coins, I <u>could buy</u> a soft drink.
correct	wrong	7. I think you <u>ought put</u> more meat in this stew.
correct	wrong	8. These boxes are so heavy. <u>May you help</u> me take them to my car?
correct	wrong	9. Paul was happy because he <u>could find</u> his keys.
correct	wrong	10. Excuse me. <u>Could you pass</u> the pepper to me?

Unit 12

Problem Words

1. *be* vs. *have*
2. *very* vs. *too*
3. *there is/are* vs. SUBJECT + *have/has*
4. subject–verb agreement
5. *almost* vs. *most*
6. *to* vs. *for*

Be vs. Have

be

The verb **be** is followed by a noun, an adjective, or a prepositional phrase.

This is a box.

It is a big box.

It is on the sofa.

have

The verb **have** is usually followed by a noun or pronoun.

Beth has a headache now.

She had it when she arrived at work.

CAREFUL! Do not use **be** when you should use **have**.

wrong: Japan is a very large population.

correct: Japan has a very large population.

144

CAREFUL! Do not use **have** with these expressions: **be hungry, be sleepy,**

be tired, be (number) years old, be lucky, be afraid, be right, be wrong,

be + TIME + in a place.

wrong: I have twenty-two years old.
correct: I am twenty-two years old.

wrong: I had five years in Germany.
correct: I was in Germany five years.

Exercise 1.   Fill in the blanks with a form of *be* or *have.* Sometimes you have to use a negative form. Follow the examples.

1. *Customer:*   Excuse me. Where _____*are*_____ men's tennis socks?

   Clerk: I'm sorry, but we _____*don't have*_____ any men's tennis socks right now.

2. *Brian:*   How long _____ you in the Middle East?

   Marcus: I _____ in Saudi Arabia two years, and I _____

   in Egypt one year.

3. *Student:*   How many questions will the test _____?

   Teacher: Fifty. The first thirty _____ true-false, so I think those

   _____ pretty easy for you.

   Student: You _____ right. True-false questions _____

   easy.

4. *Richard:*   How old _____ the president?

   Gina: I think he _____ sixty years old.

5. *Melinda:*   I found $100 today in the street.

   Tim: Wow! You _____ so lucky!

CHALLENGE   A student in your class always says, "I have twenty years," when someone asks him his age. Is this correct? Why or why not? Can you explain the answer?

Speaking Activity

Exercise 2.   Speaking Game. The whole class should play this game. If the class is large, it can be divided into groups. A group should have at least eight people. The first student starts by saying, "My name is ____, and I have __two sisters__." Use one + NOUN or any number except one + NOUN + *s*. The second student repeats the first student's information and then continues with new information. "His/her name is ____, and he/she has two sisters. My name is ____, and I have __one radio__." Continue until the last person has spoken. Then change to another *be* sentence and *have* sentence practice. Unlike with the rest of the exercises in this book, no writing is allowed!

Very vs. *Too*

very

We use **very** with an adjective or adverb to mean "more than usual" or "a higher degree of something."

A: Do you want to buy that new car?
B: I don't know. It's very expensive.
(= speaker B might buy the new car, but he or she thinks it's expensive.)

too

We use **too** with an adjective or adverb. It means "to a very high degree." We use **too** when we want to show that something is not possible.

A: Do you want to buy that new car?
B: Yes, I want to buy it, but it's too expensive.
(= speaker B will not buy the car. He or she thinks it's too expensive to buy.)

Important Note: Sometimes you will hear the expression "That's too bad." This is a special expression that means "I'm sorry to hear that." In this expression, **too bad** does not mean the same as **too expensive** or **too big.**

CAREFUL!   Do not confuse **very** and **too.** They mean different things.

wrong: I can't play tennis today because it's very hot.
correct: I can't play tennis today because it's too hot.

wrong: I enjoyed the movie. It was too good.
correct: I enjoyed the movie. It was very good.

Exercise 3.   Fill in the blanks with *too* or *very*. Follow the example.

1. *A:*   Would you like to play tennis now?

   B: Are you joking? It's ___too___ hot.

2. *A:*   Do you want some of this ice cream? It's really

          _____ good.

   B: I'm sure it is, but I'm on a diet.

3. *A:*   Is *Gone with the Wind* a good movie to see?

   B: Well, it's _____ long, so don't watch it when you're

          feeling tired.

4. *A:*   Is *Gone with the Wind* a good movie to see?

   B: Definitely not. It's _____ long.

5. *A:*   Here's a gift for you for all your help. Thanks!

   B: Wow, what is it? Could it be a watch? No, this box is _____ big for a

          watch.

   A: No, I didn't get anything like that. It's just a _____ simple gift, but I

          wanted to say thanks to you for all your help. I really do appreciate it!

6. *A:*   How was your vacation?

   B: It was _____ nice. The only bad thing is that one week was _____

          short!

7. *A:*   Look at Harry. He looks _____ sad. What's up?

   B: He got a letter with some _____ bad news in it.

8. *A:*   How's your new teacher? He seems _____ friendly.

   B: Well, he is friendly, but I can't understand his lectures. He talks _____

          fast.

Speaking Activity

Exercise 4.   Speaking Game: Book Complaints! Work with a partner. Do not let your partner see your book. This is very important! Imagine that you had to read five books. You did not like any of the books, and now you are telling a friend the reasons that you did not like the books.

Step 1.   In the column on the left, make your own list of reasons why you did not like the five books. Draw lines to make five original sentences.

Step 2.   Take turns asking *yes-no* questions about your partner's list. For example, you might ask, "Was the history book too big?" If your partner says, "No," you lose your turn. Be sure that you make some kind of note that this is not correct in the area on the right. If your partner says, "Yes," then it is still your turn to ask another question. The winner is the first partner to guess all five of his/her partner's sentences.

Your List   *Your Partner's List*

The history book was   too long.   The history book was   too long.
The math book was   too hard.   The math book was   too hard.
The science book was   too expensive.   The science book was   too expensive.
The grammar book was   too old.   The grammar book was   too old.
The literature book was   too difficult.   The literature book was   too difficult.

There Is/Are vs. SUBJECT + *Have/Has*

there is/are

We use **there is** or **there are** when we want to say that a thing or person exists. The subject comes after the verb **to be.** The usual structure is **there + is/are + SUBJECT + PLACE**.

A: What's the population of Thailand?
B: There are 32,000,000 people in Thailand.

subject + have/has

We use **SUBJECT + have/has** to express the meaning of the verb **have.** The usual structure is **SUBJECT + have/has + OBJECT** (noun or pronoun).

A: What's the population of Thailand?
B: Thailand has 32,000,000 people.

CAREFUL!   Do not use **have/has** when you should use **there is/are.**

wrong: Have many problems in my country.
correct: There are many problems in my country.
          OR: My country has many problems.

> **CAREFUL!** Do not use **is** for plural or **are** for singular.
>
> wrong: There is many problems in my country.
> correct: There are many problems in my country.

> **CAREFUL!** Do not use **do/does** for questions with **there is/there are.**
>
> wrong: Does there is a telephone in your room?
> correct: Is there a telephone in your room?
> wrong: How many letters do there are in the English alphabet?
> correct: How many letters are there in the English alphabet?

Exercise 5. Error Correction. Look at the underlined part in each sentence. If it is correct, circle *correct*. If it is wrong, circle *wrong* and write the correction above the error. Follow the example.

correct (wrong)   *There is* 1. <u>Have</u> one book on the table.

correct wrong 2. <u>There are</u> some mountains in the southern part of the country.

correct wrong 3. <u>There have</u> fifty states in the United States.

correct wrong 4. How many people <u>are there</u> in the bookstore now?

correct wrong 5. <u>It has</u> twelve inches in one foot.

correct wrong 6. Mexico <u>has</u> a long Pacific coastline.

correct wrong 7. How many days <u>has there</u> in April?

correct wrong 8. <u>There is</u> many reasons for this difficult problem.

Subject-Verb Agreement

All sentences have a *subject* and a **verb**. If the subject is singular, then the verb must be singular. If the subject is plural, then the verb must be plural.

A: How old **are** your parents?

B: My father **is** sixty, and my mother **is** sixty-two.

Sometimes there is a prepositional phrase (**PREPOSITION + OBJECT**: **of the books, on this exam**) after the subject. The object of a preposition is **NEVER** a subject.

The price of the books **is** $32.15.
S   V

The exams in this class **are** difficult!
S   V

CAREFUL! Do not mix singular and plural with subjects and verbs.

wrong: American cars uses more gasoline than Japanese cars.
correct: American cars use more gasoline than Japanese cars.

CAREFUL! Do not confuse the subject and an object of a preposition.

wrong: The war between these two countries were in 1917.
correct: The war between these two countries was in 1917.

Exercise 6.   Underline the correct verb form. Follow the example.

1. The major export product of those countries (is, are) oil.

2. What (is, are) the name of that small college in north Oklahoma?

3. Most of the people in Canada (speak, speaks) English as their first language.

4. The prime minister of Canada (speak, speaks) English and French.

5. Playing tennis well (take, takes) a lot of practice, hard work, and time.

6. The questions on the last exam (was, were) very difficult.

7. This machine (take, takes) credit cards and all bank cards.

8. There (was, were) some children in front of the store when the accident happened.

9. Shrimp and crab (doesn't have, don't have) many calories, but (it is, they are) high in protein.

10. Of all the different kinds of Cajun dishes, gumbo (is, are) my favorite.

Almost vs. *Most*

almost

We use **almost** when we want to say that something is not at the highest degree (level).

The usual structure is **almost** + **ADJECTIVE** or **almost** + **NOUN.**

A: Are you ready to go? We have to hurry up!

B: I'm almost ready. Give me two minutes.

She'll graduate soon. She's almost a doctor.

We use **almost** + **VERB** when we want to talk about something that was going to happen but did not happen in the end. Here the usual structure is **SUBJECT** + **almost** + **VERB.** Note that the verb here is usually in past tense.

A: What's wrong? You look worried.

B: I almost had a car accident just now. A child ran in front of my car to get a football. I stopped, but if I had waited one more second, . . .

most

We use **most** when we want to talk about the majority of a group. The usual structure is **most** + **NOUN** or **most** + **of** + **the** + **NOUN.**

A: Where are the students in your class from?

B: One student is from China, and a few are from Europe, but most of the students are from Latin America.

CAREFUL! Do not use **almost** when you should use **most.**

wrong: Almost Japanese people eat rice for breakfast.
correct: Most Japanese people eat rice for breakfast.

Exercise 7.   Underline the correct words. Follow the example.

1. *A:* Are the books on this table on sale?

   B: Well, (almost, <u>most</u>) of these books are on sale, but a few are not.

2. *A:* Can you spell "spinach"?

   B: I think so. s-p-i-n-n-a-c-h.

   A: Well, good try! That's (almost, most) correct, but there's only one n in spinach.

3. *A:* What time is it?

   B: It's (almost, most) 5 o'clock. Why do you ask?

4. *A:* Do you like Chinese food?

   B: Yes, but (almost, most) Chinese dishes have a lot of oil.

5. *A:* I'm going to the store. Do we need anything?

   B: Yes, get some more milk. We're (almost, most) out.

6. *A:* Do you think that (almost, most) Americans have a car?

   B: Yes, (almost, most) Americans have a car. In fact, many families have two cars!

7. *A:* How was your test?

   B: I (almost, most) failed it. My score was 72. Any score below 70 is a failing

   grade.

8. *A:* What happened to your foot?

   B: Oh, it's OK. I fell from a chair. I (almost, most) broke my foot, but it's going to

   be fine.

To vs. *For*

to
We use **to + VERB** when we want to tell the purpose of something.
(You can also say **in order to + VERB**.)

A: Why did you buy that calculator?
B: I got it to do my math homework.
(B: I got it in order to do my math homework.)

for
We use **for + NOUN** when we want to tell the purpose of something.

A: Why did you buy that calculator?
B: I got it for my math homework.

CAREFUL! Do not use **for** with verbs.

wrong: I studied two hours last night for pass today's exam.
correct: I studied two hours last night to pass today's exam.
correct: I studied two hours last night in order to pass today's exam.

Exercise 8.   Write *to* or *for* on the lines. Follow the example.

> *example:*   She bought the shirt <u>to</u> give it to Shawn. It's <u>for</u> Shawn's birthday.

1. Some people came to the United States _____ religious reasons, but others came here _____ build a better life.

2. Use this spoon _____ the soup, and use that fork _____ the salad.

3. I can't help you with the yard work tomorrow. I have to go to the library _____ get some books for a report that I have to write by Monday.

4. Please don't use these scissors _____ cut paper. If you do, it will ruin them.

5. Joseph is not here. He went to the store _____ some eggs and other groceries.

6. My grandfather gave me this watch _____ my birthday.

7. We sent a card to Shawn _____ cheer him up.

8. The coach made the players run around the field ten times _____ get them in good shape.

Exercise 9.   Multiple Choice. Circle the letter of the correct answer.

1. "How are you feeling now?"

   "Well, I _____ a little sleepy. I think I'm going to bed now."

   (A) feeling   (C) am

   (B) have   (D) need

2. "What second language do Americans speak?"

   "Actually, _____ Americans cannot speak a second language."

   (A) most   (C) most the

   (B) almost   (D) very

3. "How much _____ these books?"

   "I'm not sure. I'll have to check."

   (A) are   (C) cost

   (B) price   (D) is

4. "Do you like those doughnuts?"

   "Yes, they're _____ delicious. Did you make them?"

   (A) very   (C) most

   (B) too   (D) almost

5. "I don't know the date of that war."

   "The war between those two countries _____ in 1939."

   (A) happening   (C) were

   (B) happens   (D) was

6. "Why are we stopping?"

   "We have to get some gas. The tank is _____ empty."

   (A) too   (C) most

   (B) very   (D) almost

7. "_____ is difficult to understand."

   "Give it to me. Maybe I can understand it."

   (A) The words on the cover   (C) The language in this book

   (B) The words on the cover of this book   (D) The books in this language

8. "What's the population of Canada?"

   "Canada _____ a population of 30,500,000."

   (A) there is   (C) there are

   (B) has   (D) have

Exercise 10.   Review Test

Part 1.   Read this short passage. Underline the correct words.

This (is, are, has, have) a picture of the students in my class. My class (has, have, is, are) twenty-six students. (Almost, Most) of the students in my class (has, have, is, are) good students. However, there (is, are, has, have) one bad student. Her name is Paula Benson. She (have, has, is, are) (almost, most) always tired in class. Sometimes she (sleep, sleeps) in class, and of course the teacher (get, gets) (very, too) angry. At other times Paula (talk, talks) to some of the other students in our class. When this (happen, happens), I can't hear the teacher because the classroom (is, has, are, have) (very, too, almost, most) noisy. I (have, am) happy that I (have, am) not the teacher. She (is, has) a good teacher, but she (is, has) a really difficult job.

Part 2.   Read each sentence carefully. Look at the underlined part. If the underlined part is correct, circle the word *correct.* If it is wrong, circle the wrong part and write the correct form above.

correct	wrong	1.	This cake <u>is too</u> delicious. Please tell me how to make it.
correct	wrong	2.	I enjoyed the movie. It <u>was very</u> interesting.
correct	wrong	3.	Los Angeles, San Francisco, and Sacramento <u>there are</u> in the same state.
correct	wrong	4.	The United Nations <u>is</u> its main office in New York City.
correct	wrong	5.	The longest river in the <u>Americas is</u> the Amazon.
correct	wrong	6.	Ken, <u>you have</u> correct. Today is Joseph's birthday.
correct	wrong	7.	When I went to the store yesterday, <u>there was</u> a huge sale.
correct	wrong	8.	He and his whole family moved to Canada <u>for</u> start a new life.

Unit 13

Review

1. articles
2. *be going to* and verb tenses
3. irregular verbs
4. *how* questions

5. frequency
6. object pronouns
7. possessive
8. *other*

9. comparison
10. modals
11. problem words

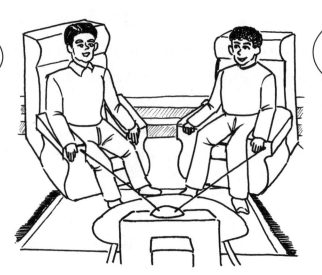

Do you **ever** watch TV?

I watch TV **almost** every night.

Exercise 1.   Articles. Fill in the blanks with *a, an, —,* or *the.*

1. *A:* Last night I saw _____ good movie.

   B: Really? What's _____ name of _____ movie?

   A: Heaven Has No Green.

   B: Maybe that is _____ movie that my sister saw _____ last week.

2. Danny and Alice are going to take _____ trip to _____ Asia _____ next summer.

   They are going to go to _____ Singapore, _____ Malaysia, _____ Thailand, and

   _____ Philippines. Danny and Alice own _____ restaurant that serves _____ Asian

   food. They will have _____ good time in Asia, but _____ main reason for their trip is

   _____ business. They are going to visit _____ many famous restaurants in these

   countries to learn more about _____ Asian cooking.

156

3. *Bill:* Tim, could you do me _____ favor? Would you please call _____ library to see

what time it closes? I need _____ book about _____ Thomas Jefferson.

Tim: Sure. I'll call right now. Why are you interested in _____ Thomas Jefferson?

Bill: I have to write _____ report about _____ him for _____ American history

class.

4. Yesterday my husband and I bought _____ new bed for _____ front bedroom. _____

price of _____ bed was only $400, so we thought it was _____ good price. We

bought it at Sullivan's Furniture Shop because we think that it's _____ best furniture

store in our area.

5. Yesterday _____ teacher in my reading class was very angry. We asked why she was so

angry, but she didn't tell us _____ reason. However, _____ friend told me _____

reason. _____ student in _____ teacher's first class copied _____ another student's

homework. Of course the teacher didn't like this.

Exercise 2. Read the time expression and then write the correct form of the verb. Follow the example.

Every Day	*Next Saturday*
1. She goes to the park.	_She's going to go to the park next Saturday._
2. She reads the newspaper.	_____
3. We visit our grandparents.	_____
Now	*Tomorrow*
4. She is eating spinach salad.	_____
5. We are going to the zoo.	_____
6. I am writing a letter to my aunt.	_____
Yesterday	*Tomorrow*
7. She studied vocabulary.	_____
8. He bought some stamps.	_____
9. They ate macaroni and cheese.	_____

Exercise 3. Irregular Verbs. Write the past tense of these verbs.

1. become _____	11. go _____	21. sell _____
2. break _____	12. hear _____	22. shut _____
3. bring _____	13. sing _____	23. build _____
4. hold _____	14. buy _____	24. hurt _____
5. catch _____	15. keep _____	25. speak _____
6. choose _____	16. know _____	26. leave _____
7. let _____	17. lose _____	27. take _____
8. drive _____	18. make _____	28. tear _____
9. fall _____	19. meet _____	29. tell _____
10. find _____	20. get _____	30. say _____

Exercise 4. *How* Questions. Read these situations. Then write a question that begins with *how* for each situation. Follow the example.

1. You want to know the number of books that are in the box.

   _____How many books are there in the box?_____

2. You want to know Carol's age.

   _____

3. You want to know if Irene goes to the movies a lot. (*Hint:* This is a frequency question.)

   _____

4. You want to know the price of this lamp.

   _____

5. You want to know the price of these two lamps.

   _____

6. You want to know the length of a tennis court.

   _____

7. You want to know if Jake was a little tired, tired, or very tired after his trip.

   _____

8. You want to know the distance from here to Mexico City.

   _____

Exercise 5. Adverbs of Frequency. Read these ten sentences. Three of them are correct, and seven have a mistake. Circle the mistakes and then write the correct form.

1. The students in my class never are absent on a test day.

2. I don't never watch TV in the morning.

3. Most of the students are usually tired after computer class.

4. Mr. Jarvis rarely is happy after he sees our exam papers.

5. Do you usually buy white bread or wheat bread?

6. The weather in New York City in January is always cold.

7. The sun shines usually for fourteen hours a day in the summer.

8. Joy arrives at the office often before eight.

9. I want to go back to that restaurant never.

10. I go shopping with sometimes Victor and Frank.

Exercise 6. Object Pronouns. Fill in the blanks with the correct subject pronoun, object pronoun, or possessive adjective.

1. *A:* Where are _____ going?

   B: I'm going to the airport. I'm going to Boston to visit _____ parents.

   A: What time is _____ flight?

   B: It leaves in about three hours.

   A: Well, can _____ help _____ with anything?

   B: No, I think I have everything, but thanks.

   A: I imagine that your parents are excited about _____ visit.

   B: Well, actually, it's a surprise. I didn't tell _____ that I'm going there.

   A: Why not?

   B: _____'s their fiftieth wedding anniversary, and I want to surprise _____.

2. *Jim:* Hi, Bob. Hi, Karen. How is _____ going?

   Karen: Hi, Jim. Everything is going OK.

   Jim: What are _____ going to do tomorrow afternoon?

   Karen: Nothing. Why?

Jim: My uncle is having a barbecue at _____ house. He told me that I could

          invite some friends. Do you want to go? _____ is really a good cook.

Bob: Thanks for inviting _____! _____ don't have plans, so we'll be there!

Karen: Where does _____ uncle live?

Jim: Actually, he lives near _____, so why don't you come to my house around

          three, and we can go to _____ house from there? How does that sound?

Exercise 7.   *One* and *Other.* Read these sentences and pay attention to the underlined parts. If the underlined part is correct, write *correct* on the line. If it is wrong, write your correction on the line. Follow the example.

1. *A:*   Would you like a doughnut?

    B: Sure. I'm hungry. Give me <u>it</u>.   *one*_____

    A: Here you go.

    B: Wow, this is great. Can I have <u>another one</u>?   *correct*_____

2. *A:*   There are four books about Washington in this

          library. Three of them are on the shelves.

    B: Where is <u>another one</u>?   _____

    A: Unfortunately, someone checked <u>one</u> out. That   _____

          person has to return <u>it</u> by the 15th.   _____

3. *A:*   Hey, there's only one pencil here, but I put two

          dozen on this table just an hour ago.

    B: Well, Mrs. Taylor, I think that some students

          took <u>the others pencils</u>.   _____

4. *A:*   How was your reading test?

    B: I failed <u>it</u>. I guess I didn't study enough.   _____

5. *A:*   What is the name of a country that begins

          with g?

    B: How about Greece or Ghana or Guam?

    A: OK. Can you think of <u>other</u>?   _____

B: Sure. There are many <u>others</u>. Guinea, Germany, and Gambia. _____

6. *A:* Well, how was the sandwich?

B: <u>It</u> was great, but I'm still hungry! _____

A: You're still hungry? If you want, I can make <u>another one</u> for you. _____

Exercise 8. Possessive Forms. Circle the letter of the usual possessive form.

1. (A) the house's roof
   (B) the roof of the house

2. (A) the game's name
   (B) the name of the game

3. (A) the car's color
   (B) the color of the car

4. (A) the table's legs
   (B) the legs of the table

5. (A) Tommy's ability
   (B) the ability of Tommy

6. (A) the child's toys
   (B) the toys of the child

7. (A) yesterday's newspaper
   (B) the newspaper of yesterday

8. (A) the desk's weight
   (B) the weight of the desk

9. (A) Mike's dictionary
   (B) the dictionary of Mike

10. (A) the students' exams
    (B) the exams of the students

Exercise 9. Comparative and Superlative. Underline the correct answers.

1. Of all the different kinds of bread in the bakery, which one is (good, better, the best)?

2. I think that those kids act (rudely, more rudely, the most rudely) than my children.

3. It is easy to see that Susan is (nicer, more nicer, the nicest) than Martha or Paul.

4. Is Diane really taller (than, from, of) her older sister?

5. Texas is (more large, larger, the largest, the most large) than California. However, Texas is not the (big, bigger, more big, biggest, most big) state. That title belongs to Alaska.

6. The movie on TV last night was not very (interesting, more interesting, the most interesting).

7. Which is (easy, easier, more easy, the easiest, the most easy) for you—science or math?

8. I'm sorry, but I can't go bowling tonight. I'm too (busy, busier, more busy, busiest, the most busy). Maybe we can go next week.

9. The weather in summer is bad, but the weather in the winter is much (bad, worse, the worst). It's so cold, and it snows all the time.

10. We bought the striped shirts instead of the white shirts because the white shirts were (more expensive, expensiver, the most expensive, the expensivest) than the striped shirts.

Exercise 10. Modals. Underline the correct word in these sentences. Sometimes more than one answer is correct.

1. *A:* Could you (taste, tastes, tasting, tasted, to taste) this soup and tell me if it's OK?

    B: Sure.

    A: Well, what do you think? (May, Can, Should, Will) I add something?

    B: You (can, must, should, would) like spicy food. This soup is pretty hot!

2. *A:* Is that a new suitcase?

    B: Yes, it is. I (will, can, am going to, ought to) fly to Boston the day after tomorrow.

    A: Oh, really? (May I, Will I, Do I have to) ask why you're going to Boston?

    B: Sure. It's not a secret. I (might, would, should) move there if I get a job at the university there.

3. *A:* Do you think we (will, had better, are going to) arrive on time?

    B: I doubt it. Look at all this traffic. There (must, should, had better) be an accident ahead.

4. *A:* (Might, Will, Can) I help you?

    B: Yes, give me a fish sandwich and large french fries.

    A: Sir, you really (had better, ought to, would, may) order the fish sandwich special lunch. For only ten cents more, you (should, can, had better) get a fish sandwich and large french fries and a large soft drink.

    B: Thanks. OK, I (am able to, ought to, going to, will) have the special lunch

          then.

5.   *A:*   How was your test? (Could you, Were you able to) answer all the questions in

          the time limit?

    B: The test was easy. I (could, was able to) answer all the questions before time

          was up.

    A: Congratulations! You (must, will, would, may, might) be really happy.

Exercise 11.   **Problem words. Underline the correct word.**

1.   *A:*   Let's go shopping.

    B: No, I'm (very, too, most, for) tired.

    A: Really?

    B: Yeah, and it's (to, too, most, almost) eight, so the mall's going to close soon.

2.   *A:*   How many students (there are, are there, it has, has it) in your English class?

    B: Only eleven. (Almost, Most) of the desks in the room are empty.

    A: Just eleven? Wow, you (have, are) so lucky! In my class, the number of students

          (are, is, has, have) thirty-two.

3.   *A:*   What (is, are) the names of the two boys on your left?

    B: One (has, is, have, are) Luke, and the other one (has, is, have, are) Kevin.

4.   *A:*   So why did you go to the store?

    B: (To, For) some popcorn. I was hungry, so I went to the store (to, for) buy

          something to eat.

Appendix of Irregular Past and Past Participles

be	was/were	been	hang	hung	hung
become	became	become	have	had	had
begin	began	begun	hide	hid	hidden
bend	bent	bent	hit	hit	hit
bind	bound	bound	hold	held	held
bite	bit	bitten	hurt	hurt	hurt
bleed	bled	bled			
blow	blew	blown	keep	kept	kept
break	broke	broken	know	knew	known
bring	brought	brought			
build	built	built	lead	led	led
buy	bought	bought	leave	left	left
			lend	lent	lent
catch	caught	caught	let	let	let
choose	chose	chosen	lie	lay	lain
come	came	come	lose	lost	lost
cost	cost	cost			
cut	cut	cut	make	made	made
			mean	meant	meant
deal	dealt	dealt	meet	met	met
dig	dug	dug			
drink	drank	drunk	put	put	put
drive	drove	driven			
do	did	done	read	read	read
draw	drew	drawn	ride	rode	ridden
			ring	rang	rung
eat	ate	eaten	run	ran	run
fall	fell	fallen	say	said	said
feed	fed	fed	see	saw	seen
feel	felt	felt	seek	sought	sought
fight	fought	fought	sell	sold	sold
find	find	find	send	sent	sent
fly	flew	flown	set	set	set
forget	forgot	forgotten	shake	shook	shaken
freeze	froze	frozen	shoot	shot	shot
			show	showed	shown
get	got	gotten	shrink	shrank	shrunk
give	gave	given	sing	sang	sung
go	went	gone	sink	sank	sunk
grow	grew	grown	sit	sat	sat

sleep	slept	slept
slide	slid	slid
speak	spoke	spoken
spend	spent	spent
stand	stood	stood
steal	stole	stolen
strike	struck	struck
swear	swore	sworn
sweep	swept	swept
swim	swam	swum
swing	swung	swung
take	took	taken
teach	taught	taught
tear	tore	torn
tell	told	told
think	thought	thought
throw	threw	thrown
understand	understood	understood
wake	woke	woken
wear	wore	worn
win	won	won
wind	wound	wound
wring	wrung	wrung
write	wrote	written

Answer Key

Unit 1

Ex. 1, p. 1: 1. aren't 2. wasn't 3. don't 4. am not 5. didn't 6. doesn't 7. didn't 8. wasn't 9. don't 10. isn't

Ex. 2, p. 2:

1.	Was		Miami and Houston in Texas?
2.	Did		New York have more people than Los Angeles?
3.	Am		Vancouver the capital of British Columbia?
4.	Do		the food at the party last night very good?
5.	Are		Washington and Lincoln born in the U.S.?
6.	Were		you make this cake yourself? It's delicious!
7.	Is		I speak too quickly?
8.	Does		I wrong?

Ex. 3, p. 2: 1. Yes, it does. No, it doesn't. 2. Yes, we were. No, we weren't. 3. Yes, they are. No, they aren't. 4. Yes, they do. No, they don't. 5. Yes, it was. No, it wasn't. 6. Yes, it is. No, it isn't. 7. Yes, you are. No, you aren't. 8. Yes, they did. No, they didn't.

Ex. 4, p. 3: 1. (A) Who went to the party last night? (B) Where did Janet and Rick go last night? (C) When did Janet and Rick go to the party? 2. What does melt mean? 3. (A) Which car belongs to John? (informal language: What car belongs to John?) (B) Whom does the red car belong to? (informal language: Who does the red car belong to?) 4. (A) What is the most abundant material in the universe? (B) What is the chemical symbol of hydrogen? 5. (A) Who called Martha? (B) Whom did Karen call? (informal language: Who did Karen call?) (C) Why did she call?

Ex. 5, p. 3: 1. that, This, those 2. this, that, that, these, Those 3. this, that

Ex. 6, p. 5: 1. some, some, any, some, some 2. some, a lot of, any 3. some, some, some, any, many, a little, some

Ex. 7, p. 7:

Simple Present	Simple Past	Present Progressive
every day	last night	at this moment
always	yesterday	this year
sometimes	the day before yesterday	today
all the time	fifteen minutes ago	this week
	in 1980	right now
		now

Ex. 8, p. 7: 1. left, came, wanted, desired, started, were, became 2. are, is, is, like, am sitting, is shining, are singing, arrived, was, aren't, went (OR am going to go), am going to eat

Ex. 9, p. 8: Student A: you were, the girl worked, the cat slept, today was, Eric needed, Joe and Pam wrote, my car used, the boys played, dinner was, Toronto had; Student B: he read, Rachel called, the cats played, we saw, the shoes cost, the teacher said, Brazil had, the boy woke, I got, the weather was

Ex. 10, p. 9: Student A: aren't, weren't, don't speak, am not, don't have, doesn't work, aren't, doesn't swim, isn't, don't do, didn't study, didn't play, isn't, wasn't, wasn't; Student B: didn't play, didn't study, isn't, doesn't like, wasn't, weren't, aren't, didn't work, don't have, am not, weren't, wasn't, weren't, doesn't have, isn't

Ex. 11, p. 11: 1. B 2. B 3. A 4. B 5. C 6. D 7. D 8. C

Ex. 12, p. 12: 1. in, at, on, in 2. at, on 3. on, at, in 4. in, in, in, in 5. in, in, in, in, at

Unit 2

Ex. 1, p. 16: 1. a 2. an 3. a 4. a 5. a 6. a 7. a 8. an 9. an 10. a 11. a 12. a 13. an 14. an 15. an 16. an 17. a 18. an 19. an 20. a 21. a 22. an 23. a 24. an 25. an 26. a 27. a 28. an 29. a 30. an

Challenge, p. 16: No, it is not correct. It is true that *umbrella, university,* and *uncle* all begin with the same letter, but these three words do not begin with the same sound. *Umbrella* and *uncle* begin with the short u sound, so we say *an* before them. *University* begins with the y sound, which is a consonant sound, so we say *a* before *university.*

Ex. 2, p. 16: 1. an 2. a 3. a 4. an 5. a 6. a 7. a 8. a 9. an 10. a 11. an 12. a 13. an 14. a 15. a

Ex. 3, p. 17: 1. —, —, a, — 2. An, —, a, —, a 3. A, —, —, —, —, — 4. —, —, an, —, —, a 5. An, —, a, — 6. —, —, an, —, —, —, —, a, —, —, — 7. A, —, —, a, —, —, a, —, —, a, — 8. —, a, —, —, a 9. —, —, —, a, —, a 10. A, —, a, —, —, a, —, —, —, —

Ex. 4, p. 18: 1. a, the 2. a, a, the, the 3. a, a, a, the, a, a, the, the, the 4. a, the, a, a, the, the, the, the, the 5. —, a, the, the, —, The, the

Ex. 5, p. 19: 1. a, the 2. a, the, a 3. a, a, The, the, a, the, the, the 4. a, the, the, the, the, the, the, a, The

Ex. 6, p. 20: 1. —, the 2. —, the 3. a, the, a, the, the, a 4. the, the, the, the, the 5. the, a, the, the 6. a, a, —, the, an, the, the

167

Ex. 7, p. 22: 1. a, the 2. the, the, — 3. the, the, a, a, the, a (OR the), a 4. the, the 5. the, the, a, the, the, the, the, the 6. the, the, —, —

Ex. 8, p. 24: 1. a, the 2. —, a, —, the, —, the 3. —, —, —, the, —, the 4. —, —, —, —, —, the, —, 5. —, —, the 6. the, the

Challenge, p. 25: It is true that *gate* is a singular count noun, so we have to use some article here. We can say *a gate* and we can say *the gate.* Both are possible. However, in this conversation, there is only one gate that is important. It is important for the passenger to go to that specific gate to catch the flight. Therefore, here we have to say *the gate.* If the passenger goes to just *a gate,* he will probably miss the flight!

Ex. 9, p. 26: 1. — 2. the 3. — 4. the 5. — 6. — 7. — 8. — 9. — 10. the 11. the 12. — 13. the 14. — 15. the 16. the 17. the 18. the 19. the 20. the 21. — 22. — 23. the 24. — 25. — 26. — 27. the 28. the 29. the 30. the

Ex. 10, p. 27: 1. — 2. — 3. the 4. the 5. the 6. — 7. — 8. the 9. the 10. — 11. the 12. — 13. the 14. — 15. the 16. the 17. the 18. the 19. the 20. the 21. — 22. the 23. — 24. — 25. — 26. the 27. the 28. — 29. — 30. —

Ex. 11, p. 27: answers will vary

Ex. 12, p. 28:

Famous Sites		Location	Facts
the	Empire State Building	New York City	• 1,250 feet tall
			• 102 floors
the	Louvre	Paris	• over a million pieces of art
	Ottawa	Canada	• capital of Canada
the	Andes Mountains	South America	• tallest mountains are 20,000 feet
the	Mississippi River	the central U.S.	• 2,340 miles long
	Mexico City	Mexico	• 15,000,000 people
the	Nile River	Egypt	• 4,145 miles long
			• longest river in Africa
the	Eiffel Tower	Paris	• built in 1889
			• 904 feet high
the	Statue of Liberty	on Ellis Island in New York City	• 301 feet high
			• 450,000 pounds
			• built in 1884

Ex. 13, p. 31: 1. B 2. A 3. D 4. A 5. B 6. C 7. D 8. C

Ex. 14, p. 32: Part 1. _—_ South Carolina is _a_ small state in <u>the</u> southeastern U.S. <u>The</u> state is shaped like _a_ small triangle. _—_ North Carolina lies to the north, and _—_ Georgia lies to the southwest. <u>The</u> Atlantic Ocean lies to the southeast.

With _a_ population of _—_ 3.5 million, _—_ South Carolina ranks 25th. About half of the people in _—_ South Carolina live in _—_ cities. <u>The</u> largest city is _—_ Columbia, which is also _the_ capital. Another important city is _—_ Charleston.

_—_ South Carolina is _—_ famous for _—_ several things. _—_ South Carolina is _an_ important manufacturing and farming state. One of its most important crops is _—_ tobacco. Many important battles of <u>the</u> American Revolution took place in _—_ South Carolina. In addition, on _—_ December 20, 1860, _—_ South Carolina became <u>the</u> first state to leave <u>the</u> U.S. _—_ Four months later, <u>the</u> Civil War between <u>the</u> northern states and <u>the</u> southern states began in _—_ Charleston. Part 2. 1. wrong (add *the:* the first show) 2. correct 3. wrong (add *the:* the same state) 4. correct 5. correct 6. wrong (omit *the:* English and French) 7. wrong (add *a:* a new blue shirt) 8. wrong (omit *the:* from gate seven)

Unit 3

Ex. 1, p. 35: 1. work 2. work 3. works 4. works 5. works 6. work 7. work 8–14. worked 15. am going to work 16. are going to work 17. is going to work 18. is going to work 19. is going to work 20. are going to work 21. are going to work

Ex. 2, p. 36: 1. I am going to study French. 2. She is going to read the newspaper. 3. They are going to do homework. 4. He is going to eat salad. 5. We are going to go to the zoo. 6. I am going to study. 7. She is going to study grammar. 8. He is going to work at the store. 9. They are going to visit Jim. 10. He is going to go to the bank. 11. We are going to play tennis. 12. I am going to read an interesting book. 13. She is going to call her mother. 14. He is going to watch a movie on TV. 15. They are going to wash their car.

Ex. 3, p. 37: (final time expressions will vary; some possibilities are: tomorrow, tonight, in two weeks, next month) 1. No, I'm (OR we're) going to cook spaghetti (+ future time expression). 2. No, she's going to call me (+ future time expression). 3. No, I'm (OR we're) going to do the homework (+ future time expression). 4. No, I'm going to be on time (+ future time expression; probable: tomorrow, tomorrow morning, from now on). 5. No, they're going to go (+ future time expression). 6. No, I'm (OR we're) going to buy a present for Keith (+ future time expression).

Ex. 4, p. 38: 1. Is Paul going to play tennis this weekend? Yes, he is. (OR No, he isn't.) When is Paul going to play tennis? This weekend. 2. Is Tina going to fly to New York in an hour? Yes, she is. (OR No, she isn't.) Where is Tina going to fly in an hour? To New York. 3. Are the girls going to watch a movie tonight? Yes, they are.

(OR No, they aren't.) When are the girls going to watch a movie? Tonight. 4. Is Victor going to work for eleven hours tomorrow? Yes, he is. (OR No, he isn't.) Who is going to work for eleven hours tomorrow? Victor. (OR Victor is.) 5. Is Laura going to study tonight? Yes, she is. (OR No, she isn't.) Why is Laura going to study tonight? She has a big test tomorrow. (OR Because she has a big test tomorrow.)

Ex. 5, p. 39: 1. played 2. are going to study 3. are going to be 4. attends 5. need 6. are listening 7. assisted 8. is raining 9. did 10. visit

Challenge, p. 39: No, it's not correct to say "I'm needing some help." We only use progressive forms for action verbs. *Need* is not an action verb.

Ex. 6, p. 39: 1. is studying 2. studied 3. studies 4. am going to study 5. did 6. do 7. are doing 8. is going to do 9. needed 10. are going to need 11. need 12. need 13. am 14. was 15. am going to be 16. am 17. Do you work 18. Are you working 19. Did you work 20. Are you going to work 21. Is it going to rain 22. Did it rain 23. Does it rain 24. Is it raining

Ex. 7, p. 41: answers will vary

Ex. 8, p. 42: 1. C 2. C 3. B 4. D 5. A 6. A 7. A 8. D

Ex. 9, p. 43: Part 1. possible answers: 1. going 2. studied 3. are going 4. to be 5. raining; is going to rain 6. do you go 7. going to; Part 2. 1. wrong (change *are going to watch* to *watched*) 2. correct 3. wrong (add *to: going to be*) 4. wrong (change *eats* to *eat*) 5. correct 6. wrong (change *Do* to *Are*) 7. wrong (change *writing* to *write*) 8. wrong (add *is: Laura is going*)

Unit 4

Ex. 1, p. 46: 1. go 2. bring 3. shut 4. steal 5. drive 6. tell 7. choose 8. send 9. fly 10. get 11. write 12. sell 13. sing 14. cut 15. swim 16. make 17. catch 18. cost 19. have 20. wake 21. say 22. give 23. grow 24. hear 25. lend 26. lose 27. fall 28. keep 29. leave 30. throw 31. wear 32. see 33. eat

Ex. 2, p. 47: 1. drank 2. gave 3. became 4. read 5. began 6. got 7. saw 8. wore 9. took 10. sat 11. broke 12. ate 13. knew 14. kept 15. spoke 16. forgot 17. tore 18. came 19. wrote 20. chose

Ex. 3, p. 47: 1. broke 2. brought 3. ate 4. did 5. woke 6. cut 7. felt 8. began 9. found 10. left 11. knew 12. meant 13. wore 14. were 15. bought 16. chose 17. went 18. rode 19. sent 20. stuck

Ex. 4, p. 48: answers will vary

Ex. 5, p. 48: 1. went, felt 2. does 3. found, gave 4. knew 5. sees 6. sit 7. writes 8. sent 9. held 10. made 11. caught 12. teaches, taught

Ex. 6, p. 49: 2. they catch, they don't catch, they caught, they didn't catch, Do they catch, Did they catch 3. we have, we don't have, we had, we didn't have, Do we have, Did we have 4. she gets, she doesn't get, she got, she didn't get, Does she get, Did she get 5. I wake, I don't wake, I woke, I didn't wake, Do I wake, Did I wake 6. you sell,

you don't sell, you sold, you didn't sell, Do you sell, Did you sell 7. you lose, you don't lose, you lost, you didn't lose, Do you lose, Did you lose 8. it takes, it doesn't take, it took, it didn't take, Does it take, Did it take 9. he speaks, he doesn't speak, he spoke, he didn't speak, Does he speak, Did he speak 10. I keep, I don't keep, I kept, I didn't keep, Do I keep, Did I keep 11. he steals, he doesn't steal, he stole, he didn't steal, Does he steal, Did he steal 12. she cuts, she doesn't cut, she cut, she didn't cut, Does she cut, Did she cut 13. we know, we don't know, we knew, we didn't know, Do we know, Did we know 14. they tear, they don't tear, they tore, they didn't tear, Do they tear, Did they tear

Ex. 7, p. 50: 1. Yes, he ate an apple. 2. No, he didn't buy a new shirt. 3. No, she didn't begin the work. 4. Yes, I saw that movie. 5. No, I didn't forget your book. 6. No, it didn't ring five times. 7. Yes, she put the shoes in the closet. 8. Yes, they broke the glass.

Challenge, p. 50: They are both wrong. *She didn't began the work* is wrong because *didn't* is past tense and *began* is past tense. You cannot put two past tense forms next to each other. *She doesn't began the work* is wrong because *doesn't* is present tense and *began* is past. The correct way to make a past negative verb form is to use *didn't* and the base or simple form of the verb. Here the correct answer is *didn't begin.*

Ex. 8, p. 50: 1. gave 2. come 3. took 4. forget 5. broke 6. were 7. began 8. give 9. ate 10. got

Ex. 9, p. 51: 1. They ate steak. 2. You told me yes. 3. He made tea. 4. I slept six hours. 5. She brought two books. 6. She bought that house in 1985. 7. He cut his right hand. 8. I heard the news this morning. 9. I chose answer A. 10. He got up at seven.

Ex. 10, p. 51: answers will vary

Ex. 11, p. 52: answers will vary

Ex. 12, p. 54: answers will vary

Ex. 13, p. 55: 1. C 2. B 3. C 4. C 5. A 6. A 7. A 8. D

Ex. 14, p. 56: Part 1. 1. choose 2. made 3. didn't understand (OR don't understand) 4. drink 5. cost; Part 2. woke (OR got), took, got, didn't eat, drove (OR took); Part 3. 1. wrong (change *isn't* to *didn't*) 2. wrong (change *Do* to *Did*) 3. correct 4. correct 5. correct 6. wrong (change *gave* to *give*) 7. wrong (change *readed* to *read*) 8. wrong (change *founded* to *found*)

Unit 5

Ex. 1, p. 58: 1. big 2. much 3. long 4. angry 5. much 6. tall 7. long 8. long 9. tall 10. many

Ex. 2, p. 59: 1. How big 2. How much 3. How long 4. How far 5. How sick 6. How tall 7. How long 8. How far 9. How much 10. How many

Ex. 3, p. 59: 1. How long do Frank and Mark work in the garden every Saturday? 2. How often does Victor drive 30 miles to his office? 3. How many miles does Victor drive to his office every day? 4. How far does Victor drive to his office every day? 5. How tall is Laura? 6. How much does Laura weigh? 7. How old is Laura? 8. How long is Tina's math class?

Challenge, p. 60: Instead of making a question with *how* + ADJECTIVE (how old, how long, how tall), it is usually possible to make another question with *what* + BE + NOUN (age, length, height). In conversation, most people use the *how* question. The *what* question is usually used in a more formal situation. For example, a police officer might ask you, "What is your height?" (or "How tall are you?") when you get your driver's license. However, someone who knows you will probably say, "How tall are you?"

Ex. 4, p. 60: answers will vary

Ex. 5, p. 63: 1. C 2. A 3. D 4. C 5. A 6. D 7. C 8. B

Ex. 6, p. 64: Part 1. 1. high 2. far 3. big 4. often 5. old 6. long 7. much 8. big (or large); Part 2. 1. correct 2. wrong (change *far* to *high*) 3. wrong (change *many* to *much*) 4. correct 5. wrong (change *usually* to *often*) 6. wrong (change *What* to *How*)

Unit 6

Ex. 1, p. 66: 1. always, 100 2. usually 3. often 4. sometimes, 50 5. rarely (OR seldom) 6. seldom (OR rarely) 7. never, 0 8. Paul 9. Florida 10. Nedra

Ex. 2, p. 67: 1. I sometimes ⟨study⟩ grammar at night. (OR Sometimes I study grammar at night. OR I study grammar at night sometimes.) 2. He usually ⟨studies⟩ vocabulary. 3. We always ⟨practice⟩ pronunciation. 4. They rarely (OR seldom) ⟨write⟩ letters to their parents. 5. You always ⟨have⟩ coffee for breakfast. 6. Jack often ⟨comes⟩ to class late. 7. Mary never ⟨sings⟩ 8. We rarely (OR seldom) ⟨speak⟩ Spanish in class. 9. They often ⟨study⟩ at night. 10. I never ⟨eat⟩ peanut butter. Bonus Question: The frequency words are before the verbs.

Ex. 3, p. 68: 1. My first class ⟨is⟩ always at 8 A.M. 2. He ⟨is⟩ usually hungry. 3. His letters ⟨are⟩ seldom (OR rarely) long. 4. Bill ⟨is⟩ never absent from Mr. Green's class. 5. Mr. Vince ⟨is⟩ usually home when the mail carrier comes. 6. They ⟨'re⟩ rarely (OR seldom) in class on Fridays. 7. I ⟨'m⟩ always nervous before a big tennis match. 8. Mary ⟨is⟩ often happy. 9. The teacher ⟨is⟩ sometimes busy in the afternoon. (OR Sometimes the teacher ⟨is⟩ busy in the afternoon. OR The teacher ⟨is⟩ busy in the afternoon sometimes.) 10. She ⟨is⟩ never sick. Bonus Question: The

frequency words are after the verb *be*.

Challenge, p. 68: No, it is definitely not correct. *Isn't* is negative, and *never* is negative. It is never OK to have two negative words together in English.

Ex. 4, p. 69: 1. is never, always seems 2. always eat 3. never study 4. is sometimes 5. seldom drinks 6. always arrive 7. is always 8. seldom speak 9. never go 10. are seldom 11. are usually 12. always has 13. is always 14. is often 15. never studies

Ex. 5, p. 70: 3. No, she doesn't. 4. Yes, he does. 5. Rarely. 6. Yes, she does. 7. Only at night.

Ex. 6, p. 70: answers will vary

Ex. 7, p. 71: answers will vary

Ex. 8, p. 72: 1. B 2. A 3. A 4. A 5. C 6. D 7. D 8. B

Ex. 9, p. 73: Part 1. 1. always arrive 2. ever go 3. sometimes wears 4. never eat 5. is always 6. rarely (OR seldom) eat 7. never (OR rarely OR seldom) makes 8. never drive; Part 2. 1. wrong (change *isn't* to *is*) 2. correct 3. correct 4. wrong (change *always you* to *you always*) 5. correct 6. correct 7. wrong (put *rarely* before *drink*) 8. correct 9. correct 10. wrong (change *do always* to *always do*)

Unit 7

Ex. 1, p. 75: 1. me 2. her 3. me, him 4. me 5. her 6. me 7. them 8. them 9. it 10. us

Ex. 2, p. 76: 1. him 2. him 3. you 4. it 5. them 6. it 7. it 8. us 9. me 10. her

Ex. 3, p. 76: 1. them 2. her 3. it 4. them 5. him 6. me 7. them 8. him 9. her 10. it, him

Ex. 4, p. 77: 1. I 2. you 3. he 4. she 5. it 6. we 7. they 8. me 9. you 10. him 11. her 12. it 13. us 14. them 15. my 16. your 17. his 18. her 19. its 20. our 21. their

Ex. 5, p. 77: 1. I 2. him 3. Their 4. They 5. She, her 6. We, our 7. We 8. He, He 9. It 10. you

Ex. 6, p. 77: 1. She, him 2. He, them 3. He, her 4. She, them 5. They, it 6. We, you 7. they, their, them 8. we, our, us 9. he, his, him 10. We, it

Ex. 7, p. 78:

Last night my wife and ⟨me⟩ [I] had dinner at a restaurant not far from ⟨us⟩ [our] home. We both

enjoy going there very much because it is a small, friendly place. We go there often, and the people

there know ⟨our⟩ [us] Last night the service was not very good. We had to wait a long time before a

waiter came to our table. He was very nice, but he didn't do a very good job. I ordered chicken

with mushrooms, but ⟨him⟩ [he] brought me chicken with cream sauce. My wife got ⟨its⟩ [her] main course OK,

but he put the wrong kind of salad dressing on her salad. We were not happy with the waiter, but

we didn't say anything to ⟨them⟩ [him]. We just ate what ⟨him⟩ [he] brought us. Because of these things, we

didn't leave a big tip.

Ex. 8, p. 78: 1. X (change *me* to *my* and *my* to *me*) 2. C 3. X (change *They are* to *It is*) 4. X (change *they* to *them*) 5. X (change *He* to *She* and *her* to *him*) 6. C 7. X (change *he* to *him*) 8. X (change *Them* to *They*) 9. C 10. X (change *us* to *our*) 11. C 12. C

Ex. 9, p. 79: Student A: them, it, it, it, them, it, them, them, it, them; Student B: them, them, it, them, them, it, it, them, it, it

Ex. 10, p. 80: 1. B 2. C 3. A 4. C 5. D 6. B 7. C 8. D

Ex. 11, p. 81: Part 1. 1. it, him 2. us 3. it 4. her 5. me; Part 2. 1. wrong (change *them* to *it*) 2. correct 3. wrong (change *she* to *her*) 4. wrong (change *her* to *him*) 5. correct 6. correct 7. correct 8. wrong (change *I* to *me*) 9. wrong (change *we* to *us*) 10. correct

Unit 8

Ex. 1, p. 82: 1. it, it 2. it 3. one 4. one 5. it, it 6. one 7. one, it 8. It

Ex. 2, p. 84: 1. another 2. Others 3. the other 4. another 5. the others 6. other 7. other 8. others 9. other 10. the other

Ex. 3, p. 85: 1. another one 2. the other one 3. the other one 4. another one 5. the other one 6. another one 7. The other one 8. another one 9. the other one 10. another one, the other one

Ex. 4, p. 86: 1. another one, the other one 2. the other one 3. the other one 4. others 5. the others 6. the other one 7. others 8. other 9. the other one 10. the other one 11. others 12. Another one, others

Ex. 5, p. 87: 1. other 2. Another one 3. others 4. the other one 5. the other one 6. others 7. Another one, others 8. the other one 9. other 10. the other one 11. another one 12. the other one

Challenge, p. 87: The correct answer is *the other one*. There are three kittens. Two of them are light brown. Now we only have one cat left. This is not an example of one more. It is the only kitten that is left. Therefore, the correct answer is *the other one*.

Ex. 6, p. 88: 1. A We cannot say the other one because there is only one group of sandwiches. It is possible to take another trip to Miami. 2. B Others means other people. We cannot say other when we should say another book. 3. B Another teacher is correct. It is not possible to say other glass because glass is singular. We should say another glass. 4. A It is not possible to say the another ones for two reasons. First, we cannot use the with an. Second, another is singular and ones is plural. This combination is impossible. 5. B We cannot use another with a plural noun such as

numbers. 6. B Plate is a count noun, so we should say another plate.

Ex. 7, p. 89: 1. B 2. B 3. C 4. C 5. A 6. C 7. A 8. B

Ex. 8, p. 90: Part 1. 1. it 2. other 3. One, others 4. the other one 5. another 6. The other 7. the others 8. it; Part 2. 1. wrong (change *one* to *it*) 2. correct 3. wrong (change *others* to *other*) 4. correct 5. wrong (change *the another one is* to *the others are*) 6. correct 7. wrong (change *others* to *other*) 8. wrong (change *other* to *another*)

Unit 9

Ex. 1, p. 93: 1. B 2. A (or B) 3. B 4. B 5. A 6. A 7. A 8. B 9. A 10. A

Ex. 2, p. 93: 1. Keith's car 2. the cover of the box 3. the child's toy 4. John's pencil 5. the woman's ring 6. today's newspaper 7. the point of the pencil 8. Tim's car 9. the beginning of the story 10. Mr. Smith's tie 11. tomorrow's homework 12. the city's problem (OR the problem of the city) 13. Ned's house 14. the secretary's work 15. Andrea's hobby

Ex. 3, p. 94: 1. Keith's car is green. 2. Jim's pencil is on the table. (OR The pencil on the table is Jim's. OR The pencil on the table is Jim's pencil.) 3. Jennifer's ring is gold. 4. Mark's books are on the desk by the door. 5. Mr. Nelson's coins are very old. 6. Dr. Guilford's nice office is at the corner of Green Street and Lincoln Avenue.

Ex. 4, p. 95: Student A: George's new house, Karen's English, tonight's homework, the color of the house, the queen of England; Student B: Jack's story, today's lunch, the price of this shirt, the name of my cat (OR my cat's name), the cover of the book

Challenge, p. 95: The teacher wasn't happy with the student's explanation because it is wrong. It is not true that you can always use *of* for possession. *Of* is only used for things. For example, we say *the name of the book* or *the price of that sofa*. We don't say *the book's name* or *the sofa's price*. The student also said "If you want, you can also use *'s* for people." No, this is not correct. It sounds like you have a choice, but you don't. We have to use *'s* for people. We say *Bob's car* and *Anna's house*. We cannot say *the car of Bob* or *the house of Anna*.

Ex. 5, p. 96: answers will vary

Ex. 6, p. 96: answers will vary

Ex. 7, p. 97: answers will vary

Ex. 8, p. 98: 1. B 2. C 3. D 4. A 5. A 6. C 7. B 8. B

Ex. 9, p. 99: Part 1. Luke's house; Luke's house; the color of Luke's house; the size of the house; The price of the house

Ex. 9, p. 100: Part 2

This book is very interesting. The name of the book is *The Dead Body*. It is about a

                  name of the town

murder in a small town. The ⟨town's name⟩ is Brookley.

                                        price of the book

   I bought this book at the bookstore on Green Street. The ⟨book's price⟩ was $27. I don't

think this book is expensive. The price of the book is all right.

                              Gibson's first book

   The Dead Body was written by Meg Gibson. This is not ⟨the first book of Gibson⟩ She

                The name of that book

wrote another book that was very famous ⟨That book's name⟩ is *The Magic Monster in the*

Mountain. The pronunciation of this title is a little difficult for some people.

                              Gibson's

   Gibson's books are very interesting. I hope you will read ⟨Gibsons⟩ books some day.

Ex. 9, p. 100: Part 3. 1. wrong (Mary and Jan's class) 2. wrong (the price of this cake) 3. correct 4. correct 5. wrong (the name of this ice cream) 6. correct 7. wrong (John's last day)

Unit 10

Ex. 1, p. 103: 1. (√) 2. (√) 3. ( ) 4. ( ) 5. (√) 6. (√) 7. ( ) 8. ( ) 9. ( ) 10. (√) 11. (√) 12. ( )

Ex. 2, p. 103: 1. taller than 2. more expensive than 3. better than 4. more carefully than 5. older than 6. worse than 7. more intelligent than 8. longer than 9. farther than 10. heavier than

Ex. 3, p. 104: 1. (√) 2. ( ) 3. (√) 4. (√) 5. (√) 6. ( ) 7. ( ) 8. (√) 9. (√) 10. (√) 11. ( ) 12. (√)

Ex. 4, p. 104: 1. the most expensive 2. the fastest 3. the most expensive 4. the most delicious 5. the most convenient 6. the largest

Ex. 5, p. 105: 1. taller, the tallest 2. more careful, the most careful 3. better, the best 4. nicer, the nicest 5. smarter, the smartest 6. farther, the farthest 7. more slowly, the most slowly 8. more rapidly, the most rapidly 9. worse, the worst 10. more quickly, the most quickly

Ex. 6, p. 105: 1. A 2. A 3. B 4. A 5. A 6. B 7. A 8. A 9. B 10. B

Ex. 7, p. 106: 1. taller than, the tallest 2. the best 3. the happiest 4. interesting, more interesting 5. more difficult 6. the prettiest 7. nice, nicer than 8. bad, worse 9. easier than 10. cold, colder than 11.

tall, the tallest, taller than, taller than 12. large, larger than, the largest, The largest

Ex. 8, p. 107: er and *the . . . est:* tired, smooth, strong, cheap, warm, heavy, nice, deep, fast, noisy, salty, friendly, sharp, late, dull, high, crunchy, early; *more and the most:* modern, slowly, careful, exciting, expensive, serious, quickly, quiet, intelligent, comfortable, badly, crowded, dangerous, delicious, interesting; irregular: good/better/the best, bad/worse/the worst, far/farther/the farthest

Ex. 9, p. 107: 1. D 2. C 3. B 4. A 5. B 6. C 7. B 8. D

Ex. 10, p. 108: Part 1. harder, more expensive, the most expensive, better, the best, nicer, more interesting

Ex. 10, p. 109: Part 2

Last week I read a book called *Victory*. It was very interesting. However, I just finished

                                more

reading a book called *Behind the Wall*. I think this book was ⟨most⟩ interesting than *Victory*. Both

                                     better

books are about the war in the early 1900s, but *Behind the Wall* was ⟨more better.⟩

   Some people don't want to read *Behind the Wall* because it's so long. *Victory* was a long

                                  than

book. It has 350 pages, but *Behind the Wall* is longer ⟨from⟩ *Victory*. *Behind the Wall* has 468

pages.

                                 easier

   I also enjoyed *Behind the Wall* because it is ⟨more easy⟩ to read. The author wrote very

clearly. Some parts of *Behind the Wall* were difficult to understand, but this was not true with

Victory.

Ex. 10, p. 109: Part 3. 1. correct 2. correct 3. correct 4. wrong (change *from* to *than*) 5. wrong (add *the* before *brightest*) 6. wrong (omit *more: stronger than*)

Unit 11

Ex. 1, p. 113: 1. B 2. A, C 3. B 4. A, C 5. A, B, C

Ex. 2, p. 114:

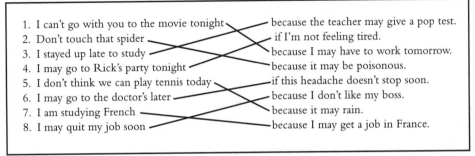

1. I can't go with you to the movie tonight — because it may rain.
2. Don't touch that spider — because it may be poisonous.
3. I stayed up late to study — because the teacher may give a pop test.
4. I may go to Rick's party tonight — if I'm not feeling tired.
5. I don't think we can play tennis today — if this headache doesn't stop soon.
6. I may go to the doctor's later — if this headache doesn't stop soon.
7. I am studying French — because I may get a job in France.
8. I may quit my job soon — because I don't like my boss.

Ex. 3, p. 115: 1. May I sit here? 2. You may check out three books if you have a library card. (OR If you have a library card, you may check out three books.) 3. May we take photographs here? 4. May I use your telephone to call my mom? 5. You may use this computer to send an e-mail message to her if you want. (OR If you want, you may use this computer to send an e-mail message to her.)

Ex. 4, p. 116: 1. aren't able to 2. aren't able to 3. can speak 4. aren't able to, can 5. can't drive

Ex. 5, p. 117: answers will vary

Ex. 6, p. 118: answers will vary

Ex. 7, p. 119: 1. D 2. A 3. C 4. F 5. H 6. B 7. E 8. G

Challenge, p. 119: In formal English, we use *may* for permission. We say, "May I sit here?" or "May I use your telephone?" However, in informal language, people use *can* for permission. You might ask your friend, "Can I sit here?" or "Can I use your telephone?" The student says that his friends say *may* instead of *can*. This is not surprising because it is probably informal language among friends.

Ex. 8, p. 120: A. Could you please tell me the location of the museum? B. Could you please bring me a salad and a glass of iced tea? (OR Could you please bring me a glass of iced tea and a salad?) C. Could you please put this bag under the seat in front of you during takeoff? D. Could you please explain that word again? E. Could you please give me five forty-cent stamps? F. Could you please tell me the price of this watch? G. Could you please open the window? Part 2. 1. F 2. B 3. G 4. D 5. C 6. A 7. E

Ex. 9, p. 122: 1. correct 2. wrong (was able to find; OR found) 3. correct 4. correct 5. correct 6. wrong (was able to talk; OR talked) 7. correct 8. correct 9. wrong (was able to give; OR gave) 10. wrong (was able to get; OR got)

Ex. 10, p. 123: answers will vary

Ex. 11, p. 125: answers may vary 1. If I left in the morning, I could save $70. 2. If I had a car or a bicycle, I would go to the park. 3. If I had a dictionary, I could look up the past tense of ride. 4. If Victor had a phone, I could call him. 5. If this food weren't so salty, I could eat it.

Ex. 12, p. 126: 1. are you going to 2. will 3. will; OR is going to 4. am going to 5. will 6. am going to 7. will; OR am going to (if this was a planned action) 8. will; OR is going to 9. will 10. will

Ex. 13, p. 127:

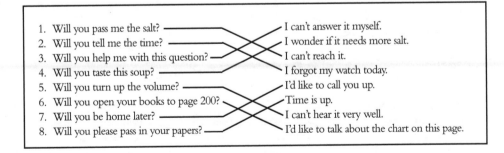

1. Will you pass me the salt? — I can't reach it.
2. Will you tell me the time? — I forgot my watch today.
3. Will you help me with this question? — I can't answer it myself.
4. Will you taste this soup? — I wonder if it needs more salt.
5. Will you turn up the volume? — I can't hear it very well.
6. Will you open your books to page 200? — I'd like to talk about the chart on this page.
7. Will you be home later? — I'd like to call you up.
8. Will you please pass in your papers? — Time is up.

Ex. 14, p. 128: 1. does Pedro want, would Pedro like 2. want, would like 3. want, would like 4. Do you want, Would you like 5. do you want, would you like 6. Do you want, Would you like 7. want, would like 8. Does the teacher want, Would the teacher like

Ex. 15, p. 129: answers will vary

Ex. 16, p. 131: answers will vary

Ex. 17, p. 133: answers will vary

Ex. 18, p. 134: possible answers: 1. it should be soft (OR done; OR cooked) 2. it should be higher (OR it should be for two weeks) 3. should have ten 4. should be eighty-one 5. should be cooler (OR should not be so hot) (*Note: ought to* can be used in place of *should* in this exercise.)

Ex. 19, p. 136:

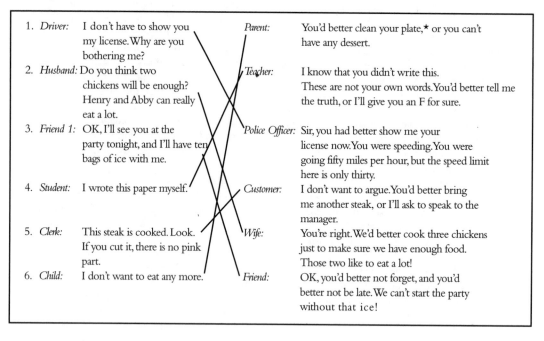

1. *Driver:*	I don't have to show you my license. Why are you bothering me?	*Parent:*	You'd better clean your plate,★ or you can't have any dessert.
2. *Husband:*	Do you think two chickens will be enough? Henry and Abby can really eat a lot.	*Teacher:*	I know that you didn't write this. These are not your own words. You'd better tell me the truth, or I'll give you an F for sure.
3. *Friend 1:*	OK, I'll see you at the party tonight, and I'll have ten bags of ice with me.	*Police Officer:*	Sir, you had better show me your license now. You were speeding. You were going fifty miles per hour, but the speed limit here is only thirty.
4. *Student:*	I wrote this paper myself.	*Customer:*	I don't want to argue. You'd better bring me another steak, or I'll ask to speak to the manager.
5. *Clerk:*	This steak is cooked. Look. If you cut it, there is no pink part.	*Wife:*	You're right. We'd better cook three chickens just to make sure we have enough food. Those two like to eat a lot!
6. *Child:*	I don't want to eat any more.	*Friend:*	OK, you'd better not forget, and you'd better not be late. We can't start the party without that ice!

Ex. 20, p. 137:

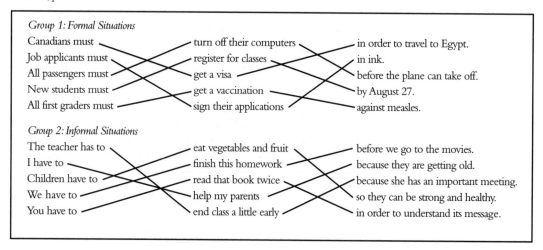

Group 1: Formal Situations

Canadians must — turn off their computers — in order to travel to Egypt.
Job applicants must — register for classes — in ink.
All passengers must — get a visa — before the plane can take off.
New students must — get a vaccination — by August 27.
All first graders must — sign their applications — against measles.

Group 2: Informal Situations

The teacher has to — eat vegetables and fruit — before we go to the movies.
I have to — finish this homework — because they are getting old.
Children have to — read that book twice — because she has an important meeting.
We have to — help my parents — so they can be strong and healthy.
You have to — end class a little early — in order to understand its message.

Ex. 21, p. 138: answers will vary

Ex. 22, p. 139: 1. don't have to choose (OR read), must not choose, must not be (OR have), doesn't have to be 2. don't have to, must not take, don't have to come, must not wait

Ex. 23, p. 140: 1. It must be blue. 2. He must be tired (OR exhausted). 3. It must be a new vase. 4. She must be happy (OR surprised).

Ex. 24, p. 141: 1. B 2. C 3. C 4. A 5. C 6. A 7. C 8. A

Ex. 25, p. 143: Part 1. 1. are you going to 2. may 3. has to 4. might 5. shouldn't 6. ought to 7. should 8. must; Part 2. 1. correct 2. wrong (have to) 3. wrong (Children cannot use *had better* to their parents. One possible way to change the sentence is just to say "The house looks so dirty.") 4. correct 5. correct 6. correct 7. wrong (ought to put; OR should put) 8. wrong (Can you help; OR Would you help) 9. wrong (was able to find; OR found) 10. correct

Unit 12

Ex. 1, p. 145: 1. are, don't have 2. were, was, was 3. have, are (OR will be), will be (OR are), are, are 4. is, is 5. are

Challenge, p. 145: In English, we use *be* to express age. We say, "I am twenty years old." However, in some languages, such as French and Spanish, they say, "I have twenty years." However, this is not correct in English. What about your language? Does your language use *be* or *have* or a different verb?

Ex. 2, p. 146: answers will vary

Ex. 3, p. 147: 1. too 2. very 3. very 4. too 5. too, very 6. very, too 7. very, very 8. very, too

Ex. 4, p. 148: answers will vary

Ex. 5, p. 149: 1. wrong (There is) 2. correct 3. wrong (There are) 4. correct 5. wrong (There are) 6. correct 7. wrong (are there) 8. wrong (There are)

Ex. 6, p. 150: 1. is 2. is 3. speak 4. speaks 5. takes 6. were 7. takes 8. were 9. don't have, they are 10. is

Ex. 7, p. 151: 1. most 2. almost 3. almost 4. most 5. almost 6. most, most 7. almost 8. almost

Ex. 8, p. 153: 1. for, to 2. for, for 3. to 4. to 5. for 6. for 7. to 8. to

Ex. 9, p. 153: 1. C 2. A 3. A 4. A 5. D 6. D 7. C 8. B

Ex. 10, p. 155: Part 1. is, has, Most, are, is, is, almost, sleeps, gets, very, talks, happens, is, too, am, am, is, has; Part 2. 1. wrong (is very) 2. correct 3. wrong (are) 4. wrong (has) 5. correct 6. wrong (you are) 7. correct 8. wrong (to)

Unit 13

Ex. 1, p. 156: 1. a, the , the, the, — 2. a, —, —, —, —, —, the, a, —, a, the, —, —, — 3. a, the, a, —, —, a, —, — 4. a, the, The, the, a, the 5. the, the, a, the, A, the, —

Ex. 2, p. 157: 1. She is going to go to the park. 2. She is going to read the newspaper. 3. We are going to visit our grandparents. 4. She is going to eat spinach salad. 5. We are going to go to the zoo. 6. I am going to write a letter to my aunt. 7. She is going to study vocabulary. 8. He is going to buy some stamps. 9. They are going to eat macaroni and cheese.

Ex. 3, p. 158: 1. became 2. broke 3. brought 4. held 5. caught 6. chose 7. let 8. drove 9. fell 10. found 11. went 12. heard 13. sang 14. bought 15. kept 16. knew 17. lost 18. made 19. met 20. got 21. sold 22. shut 23. built 24. hurt 25. spoke 26. left 27. took 28. tore 29. told 30. said

Ex. 4, p. 158: 1. How many books are there in the box? 2. How old is Carol? 3. How often does Irene go to the movies? 4. How much does this lamp cost? (OR How much is this lamp?) 5. How much do these two lamps cost? (OR How much are these two lamps?) 6. How long is a tennis court? 7. How tired was Jake after his trip? 8. How far is Mexico City from here? (OR How far is it from here to Mexico City?)

Ex. 5, p. 159: 1. never are = are never 2. don't never = don't ever OR never 3. correct 4. rarely is = is rarely 5. correct 6. correct 7. shines usually = usually shines 8. Joy arrives at the office often = Joy often arrives at the office 9. never = I never want to go back to that restaurant 10. sometimes = I sometimes go

Ex. 6, p. 159: 1. you, my, your, I, you, your, them, It, them 2. it, you, his, He, us, We, your, me, his

Ex. 7, p. 160: 1. one, correct 2. the other one, it, correct 3. the other pencils 4. correct 5. another, correct 6. correct, correct

Ex. 8, p. 161: 1. B 2. B 3. B 4. B 5. A 6. A 7. A 8. B 9. A 10. A

Ex. 9, p. 161: 1. the best 2. more rudely 3. nicer 4. than 5. larger, biggest 6. interesting 7. easier 8. busy 9. worse 10. more expensive

Ex. 10, p. 162: 1. taste, Should, must 2. am going to, May I, might 3. will OR are going to, must 4. Can, ought to, can, will 5. Could you OR Were you able to, was able to, must

Ex. 11, p. 163: 1. too, almost 2. are there, Most, are, is 3. are, is, is 4. For, to

Final Test

Name_____   Date_____

This test has 24 questions. You will receive 1 point for circling the error
and 1 point for correcting the error. Perfect score = 48.
Your score: _____/48 = _____%
(70% minimum recommended passing)

Each sentence contains one error. Circle the error and write a correction on the line. If
your answer is long, you may write it above the sentence.

example: ____have____   I (has) a book.

Part 1

1. _____   Where lives John?

2. _____   I bought very good dictionary at the bookstore yesterday.

3. _____   Two students going to travel to New York City next

   week.

4. _____   My brother goed to London in 1993.

5. _____   How age is the teacher?

6. _____   We don't never eat pizza for breakfast.

7. _____   This big present is for she.

8. _____   Please give me other pencil. This one is not very good.

9. _____   I visited the home of John and Mary last night.

10. _____   I think Japanese cars are best than American cars.

11. _____   I can't to go with you to the park tomorrow.

12. _____   The students in my grammar class is from many different

    countries.

Part 2

1. _____   Where lives the president of the United States?

2. _____   I am very interested in the modern art.

3. _____   Jill and I are going play tennis together tomorrow.

4. _____   Did you gave the books to Jim and Nedra?

5. _____ How long are you? Almost six feet?

6. _____ Luke arrives always late to class.

7. _____ Do Mark and Bob have their books with their?

8. _____ Some people like tea; others people prefer coffee.

9. _____ Do you know this ice cream's name?

10. _____ Alaska is the most large state in the United States.

11. _____ Are you can play tennis very well?

12. _____ The reason for these new laws are very simple.

Diagnostic Test

Name_____ Date_____

Directions: Mark an X on the letter of the correct answer. Mark all answers on this sheet.

1a.	(A) (B) (C) (D)	1b.	(A) (B) (C) (D)	_____
2a.	(A) (B) (C) (D)	2b.	(A) (B) (C) (D)	_____
3a.	(A) (B) (C) (D)	3b.	(A) (B) (C) (D)	_____
4a.	(A) (B) (C) (D)	4b.	(A) (B) (C) (D)	_____
5a.	(A) (B) (C) (D)	5b.	(A) (B) (C) (D)	_____
6a.	(A) (B) (C) (D)	6b.	(A) (B) (C) (D)	_____
7a.	(A) (B) (C) (D)	7b.	(A) (B) (C) (D)	_____
8a.	(A) (B) (C) (D)	8b.	(A) (B) (C) (D)	_____
9a.	(A) (B) (C) (D)	9b.	(A) (B) (C) (D)	_____
10a.	(A) (B) (C) (D)	10b.	(A) (B) (C) (D)	_____
11a.	(A) (B) (C) (D)	11b.	(A) (B) (C) (D)	_____
12a.	(A) (B) (C) (D)	12b.	(A) (B) (C) (D)	_____

TEACHER ONLY

SCORING THE TEST

The question numbers represent the unit numbers in the book. For example, 7a and 7b are two questions about the material in unit 7.

Circle the unit numbers below that had two mistakes. These units should be done first.

Underline the units that had one mistake. These units should be done next.

Units: 1 2 3 4 5 6 7 8 9 10 11 12

Diagnostic Test Questions

1a. "How was the party?"

"I don't know. I _____ because I didn't feel well."

(A) didn't go   (C) didn't went

(B) don't go   (D) don't went

2a. "I bought a bag of potato chips yesterday. Where is it?"

"I'm sorry, but Susan and I ate _____ last night."

(A) some chips   (C) the chips

(B) chips   (D) a chips

3a. "It's so hot in here!"

"Yes, it is. I _____ turn on the air conditioner."

(A) am going to   (C) going to

(B) am going   (D) be going

4a. "_____ to Miami?"

"Yes, we took Northwest Airlines."

(A) Do you fly   (C) Did you fly

(B) Did you flew   (D) Do you flew

5a. "How _____?"

"I'm not very sure, but he's taller than I am."

(A) tall is William   (C) tall William is

(B) William is tall   (D) William tall is

6a. "Do you like sports?"

"Yes, very much. _____ tennis Tuesday and Thursday nights."

(A) I always play   (C) always I play

(B) I play always   (D) always play I

7a. "Is this your book, or is it John's?"

"It was mine, but I gave it to _____ yesterday."

(A) he   (C) his

(B) them   (D) him

8a. "Hey, this sandwich is great!"

"Would you like _____ one? There are some on the table."

(A) another

(C) other

(B) the other

(D) others

9a. "Did you buy the table?"

"No, I didn't. _____ were not strong."

(A) The legs the table

(C) The table's legs

(B) The legs of the table

(D) The table of the legs

10a. "None of the boys wants to work."

"That is true, but Paul and Joseph are _____."

(A) more lazy

(C) the most lazy

(B) lazy

(D) the laziest

11a. "Are you going to the party tomorrow night?"

"Yes, I'll be there, but I _____ a little late."

(A) can to arrive

(C) can arrive

(B) might to arrive

(D) might arrive

12a. "Let's go bowling."

"I went bowling last night, and I played tennis this morning. I'm _____ to do anything now. Maybe tomorrow, OK?"

(A) too tired

(C) tired too

(B) very tired

(D) tired very

1b. "Can you lend me ten dollars until tomorrow?"

"I'm really sorry, but I don't _____ money right now, so I can't lend you any."

(A) has much

(C) have much

(B) has many

(D) have many

2b. "Do you read a lot?"

"Yes, I do. I'm reading a very good book now. _____ is *Jungle*."

(A) The title of a book

(C) The title of the book

(B) A title of a book

(D) A title of the book

3b. "You look sick. Are you feeling OK?

"No, I'm not. _____ to the doctor's office."

(A) I will go   (C) I'm go to going

(B) I am go   (D) I'm going to go

4b. "Did you finish the homework?"

"Yes, I read all the books, and I _____ the final report."

(A) write   (C) wrote

(B) was write   (D) was wrote

5b. "_____ did you stay in Germany?"

"We were there three years."

(A) What time   (C) How much

(B) What years   (D) How long

6b. "What do you usually do for your father's birthday?"

"My brothers and sisters and I _____ him to a nice restaurant for a big dinner.

I think he likes to see all of us together again."

(A) take always   (C) take never

(B) always take   (D) never take

7b. "Can you please give this letter to Mr. and Mrs. Taylor?"

"Sure, I'll give _____ this afternoon."

(A) them to it   (C) their to it

(B) it to them   (D) it to their

8b. "May I use this green pen?"

"No, that one doesn't write well. Please use _____."

(A) it   (C) one

(B) another one   (D) the other

9b. "Who is that boy in the green sweater?"

"_____ is Vic Richards. He's new."

(A) The boy's name   (C) The name of the boy

(B) The name's boy   (D) The boy of the name

10b. "Which do you think is _____ for an English speaker to learn—Arabic or Chinese?"

"The answer is definitely Chinese. The writing and pronunciation are extremely hard."

(A) more hard   (C) the most hard

(B) more difficult   (D) the most difficult

11b. "Please type this for me."

"Sorry, I _____."

(A) am not able type   (C) cannot type

(B) can't to type   (D) am not able typing

12b. "There are twelve provinces in Canada, right?"

"No, that's wrong. Canada _____ twelve provinces."

(A) don't has   (C) there isn't

(B) doesn't have   (D) there aren't